World renowned dog trainer [...] years working with dogs and ho[...]ques. Previously he worked as a de[...]heme parks in the West Country as well as running one of the biggest training and breeding centres in Devon. He now lives in a rural valley in South Wales with his dogs, devoting his time to understanding what motivates them and writing books to help other owners become their dog's best friend.

His first book, *The Dog Whisperer: How to Train Your Dog Using Its Own Language*, was published by Headline in 2008.

Praise for THE DOG WHISPERER:

'*The Dog Whisperer* details [Sims's] strategies, providing a comprehensive masterclass in pooch training that can make any man (or woman) a dog's best friend' Shari Low, *Daily Record*

'It reads so easily and works so well with all the examples of dogs you have met and worked with . . . It will help so many people understand their dogs better and be a better owner' Julie Hill, presenter of Dogcast Radio

'An excellent book about training your dog. The method requires a considerable amount of time and patience but pays dividends. Unusually for a book of the type it is very readable with some wonderful cartoons which left me howling with laughter. Highly recommended' Sue Magee, *The Book Bag*

'Anyone who works with, lives with, and cares about dogs will enjoy and learn from this book. It is informative, entertaining and real in that the author does not pretend to have always got everything right. It has humility and humour, and a great deal of wisdom' Work Wonders 'Woof' on Amazon.co.uk

'Get this if you want to read a witty, touchingly sentimental, practical and rewarding book that will help you train your dog. Also, though, it's a superb read for those without a four-legged friend; it tells us how much can be achieved with a healthy dose of tolerance, compassion and time . . . two books in one. A bargain' R. Jones on Amazon.co.uk

GIVE A DOG A HOME

How to make your rescue dog a happy dog

Illustrations by Graeme Sims

GRAEME SIMS
the man who speaks dog

headline

By Graeme Sims and available from Headline

The Dog Whisperer
Give a Dog a Home

First published in 2009 by
HEADLINE PUBLISHING GROUP

First published in paperback in 2010 by
HEADLINE PUBLISHING GROUP

1

Cataloguing in Publication Data is available from the British Library

ISBN 978 0 7553 1704 2

Typeset in Baskerville by Avon DataSet Ltd, Bidford on Avon, Warwickshire

Printed in the UK by CPI Mackays, Chatham, ME5 8TD

Headline's policy is to use papers that are natural, renewable and recyclable
products and made from wood grown in sustainable forests. The logging and
manufacturing processes are expected to conform to the environmental
regulations of the country of origin.

HEADLINE PUBLISHING GROUP
An Hachette UK Company
338 Euston Road
London NW1 3BH

www.headline.co.uk
www.hachette.co.uk
www.graemesims.com

I dedicate this book to all of the people who rescue a dog and change its life for the better by giving it a loving home. I remember all those animals that I have loved and lost and those whose furry, warm bodies I can still stroke today.

Dear Mr Sims,

I'm so glad that you gave good advice to my 'mummy and daddy', don't they realise that I'm sensitive? I was a bit miffed that they dwelt on seemingly negative parts of my behaviour.

They didn't say how I cheer people up with my wagging tail, and that I visited David's mother, who has Alzheimer's, when she was in the local cottage hospital and visit her now in a nursing home. The patients smile and look happy when they see what a handsome chap I am!

I've stayed in hotels, where I always lie in a strategic position so that people have to comment on me. I tailor myself to them . . . I was very gentle with a lady with special needs, but got a little bit boisterous with the singer who owned dogs and horses.

I've just been to the vet as I've had a little problem with my prostate. I couldn't begin to tell you what the nice lady vet did . . . I am taking some antibiotics and returning next week. I had the last laugh, though – I cocked my leg over the vet's doorstep as I left!

Thank you, Mr Sims, you sound like a lovely man with a lovely family. I think my mummy is going to do a cross-stitch for you, it may be of a verse from the bible or of a Border collie . . . She's full of good intentions!

Lots of licks and woofs from Callum

e-mail from Angela, David and Callum via my clinic pages on www.graemesims.com and www.simssheepdogs.co.uk

Contents

Acknowledgements

I thank Val Hudson for her open, inclusive and enlightened style of management and Lorraine Jerram for her always candid and wise advice, and would like to show my appreciation here for their always-in-touch, heartening and kind support.

What a difference really nice people make!

Preface

Some people love my books and some don't. Most find the answers to the problems they are having with their dogs but a few find nothing but shadows.

There is no single blueprint. There are no carefully measured recipes here – no lists of precisely weighed ingredients or strict methods of preparation. Training a dog is not a simple matter of saying, 'take a human and a dog, and mix', it is a far more complicated business.

Successful training acknowledges that there are many types of human and at least as many types of dog and that the problems both suffer have an enormous variety of causes: multiply each by each and you will begin to appreciate my point.

The dog is not an automaton but a creature of endless variation: there is no standard and training is not confined to training sessions – it happens every minute of every day.

I can be sure of just three things:

1 That there is always a cause
2 That the gentle way can cure
3 That the dominant way merely suppresses

If you are looking for a mechanical list of 'do this and that'

that you can follow slavishly, without the need to look hard and think much, this book is not for you. In fact, if you are expecting some kind of 'read but don't think' formula, it could well be that a dog is not the perfect pet for you.

This is a good place to ask you a riddle: How is it that your dog knows that you are about to turn the television off? And what is so exciting to the dog about that event? Hopefully, reading this book will help you really *think* and solve the puzzle yourself.

The work I suggest here will have to be done by you. The thinking is for you to do. All I give you is a gentle, well-and-truly tested route which, if followed, will work.

If you can see the dog as a thinking, feeling, sentient creature well worthy of your best mental and physical efforts, then – welcome home.

Chapter One

Auld Lang Syne

Christmas is over, tribes of small (and not so small) children have ceased to run screaming from room to room. Planes, trains and cars have departed taking their young passengers with them to various points in this country and abroad. No more need for continuous surveillance. A pin dropped two rooms away would now be as a clanging bucket on cold flags, for this is the kingdom of silence.

Adults lie down in quiet, darkened rooms (metaphorically). There is a quietness just waiting to be contemplated; you can almost touch it, like gossamer. Children are like sweeties: just enough is perfect but do not eat the whole packet.

In a forgotten corner the Christmas tree, prematurely retired, lonely now and uncelebrated, droops like an almost needle-free skeleton (either because of the warmth or, perhaps, the noise?), the presents have vanished but the lights live on, still encouragingly bright, twinkling as if to say, don't forget, don't forget.

Tonight, in splendid isolation, my wife Maureen and I will watch the old year go out and a new one begin.

No doubt someone, somewhere, on television or radio, will sing *Auld Lang Syne* and stir up memories of the past and anxieties for the future. Certainty belongs to the past, hope is the future's word.

I have gone down to the kennels, as I do repeatedly, to check on the dogs.

Our kennels are built inside a double garage so there is a 'second skin' to protect against the elements. Each kennel is generously insulated as well as having central heating.

Some dogs like to sleep together while others are confirmed 'loners' so we have both single and double bedrooms. It is like a doggy hotel and I am the janitor and the provider of room service.

Bob, my oldest dog, had the canine equivalent of a stroke a few months ago. He was sick, then fell over and had to be helped to his feet and held there for some time until he recovered a degree of equilibrium. I carried him back to his kennel, panting under his weight.

I thought I would lose him there and then. For two weeks or so he was incapable of walking in a straight line, suddenly and disturbingly veering off to the left as lack of balance took hold.

We wanted to avoid all extremes, such as prolonged cold

or rain or, indeed, too much of anything. Bob's kennel central heating was switched to continuous and now, night and day, a red, warm light spills out of his house to make the whole kennel area look cosy.

At night I put his first daughter, Gemma, in to sleep with him; she is kind and will snuggle up to him all night long. Some dogs never show any awareness, or consideration, that the dog that is close to them is Mother or Father or that their companion is noticeably getting old, but Gemma treats her old dad the way I hope my daughters might treat me when I'm too old to fend for myself.

The sleeping area of each kennel measures four feet by four, the door between the outside run and the sleeping quarters is human size but has a pop hole in the middle so the dogs have easy access through their own entrance and, even though it's not really necessary, each kennel has a weather strip (vertical strips of plastic covering the pop hole) to keep the draughts out.

Bob's door is left open so that he can see what is going on. Isolating Bob will not help him as he has always lived among his own tribe and needs to see the comings and goings that are the pulse of each day. I aim for as much normality as possible but cosset as well.

Inside, he has the most luxuriously thick duvet which spills out of the kennel door like custard overflowing a pudding dish. In fact, it all looked so comfortable – the two dogs' furry faces poking out – that I popped right inside to see them.

Old Friends

I make myself comfortable on Bob's thick duvet and both dogs cuddle up to me. The infrared light glows on the featureless walls so that it looks like the inside of a spaceship and warms in a soothing way. Time is suspended, the outside world ceases to be.

Bob and Gemma's fur is warm, and they stretch and turn in the same way we humans do in order to snuggle into newly found cosy patches.

The soft light brings back memories of wet lambs and of puppies and their mums, all being mollycoddled; and of farms and barns a long way off in a place now occupied by fond reminiscences. I remember puppies nestling in deep, golden straw and that very special scent of lanolin in the wool of my sheep.

Bob, Gemma and I sit together in this timeless – almost soundless – place and I find myself wishing that this could last for evermore but knowing that life is not like that because the end has to come to all creatures, for all time.

I try to be philosophical about the limited time we all have. 'Try' is the word, 'succeed' is not. Just a little more, then a little more again would do very nicely thank you.

The only trouble with having fourteen dogs is that one day we shall lose them – or they, us. Both dogs and humans are getting old and I am fearful sometimes.

In this warm and quiet place my mind wanders backward and forward. I remember the good years as a shepherd and the sights and sounds of dogs and sheep. I remember narrow, winding lanes and how, when returning from the dip, the evening sun would turn the sheep's now yellow wool to rosy pink. And, of course, I remember each and every one of the dogs we have had. I can play them back in the film in my head with an intensity that never fails to surprise me.

I can remember sheepdog trials up in the hills of Exmoor and, in particular, I remember the sight and enormous satisfaction of Bob doing the job he loved with such style and grace.

In some ways I was good at being a shepherd and in some ways bad. I was always excused from having to weigh the lambs to go to market because I was unwilling to 'play God' – a kind of hypocrisy because, of course, I still played a part in the process.

I remember that I became more gentle
as my knowledge grew, and how – much
to the amusement of harder shepherds –
I began to regard my dogs as equal partners
and to treat them accordingly.

When we moved to this beautiful Welsh valley – where we still live – I met a sheep farmer who has since become a good friend. One day (before we got to know each other) we stood chatting in his farmyard as the sun went down and he asked me a series of questions.

'How many sheep do you have?' he began.

I told him, then added that they were all rams and were now retired. The conversation went on with a question about our ducks. My answer included the fact that they were retired, too.

7

The last question was about the dogs. I can't remember accurately what the query was but it was based around, did we still breed them and would I have any more new dogs. Whatever the exact words, the essence of my answer was 'no'.

'So you could say that you are going nowhere,' he observed candidly.

His pragmatic response came as quite a shock – probably because it contained more than a thread of truth.

I thought long and hard about what he had said and determined that if a similar discussion should take place in future, I would be ready with a response that would accurately describe the reality of my situation.

> *My dogs, sheep and ducks are more than functional, more than just tools.*

During the many years that I spent working in theme parks, demonstrating the working intelligence of sheepdogs, the animals provided most of the spectacle. People came to watch me *and* my animals – whether I was training, herding or feeding them – and those people paid entrance money which I received a portion of. My furry, woolly and feathered creatures were fellow actors in the entertainment we offered, as well as being friends with whom I spent much of my time.

What was I supposed to do, then? Offer no more than a cynical 'thank you' before condemning my former troupers to an untimely end? Or pay my friends back properly with a long and hopefully comfortable retirement?

I suppose, to a farmer who takes sheep to market and comes back with money it could easily look as if we are 'going nowhere' because, on the outside, nothing tangible seems to be happening. But from where I stand we are, in fact, going to a very important somewhere as with each day I learn new things about the way dogs, and other creatures, communicate.

To some, I must look like an artist who sits forever before the same blank canvas yet never seems to apply the paint. But before we can teach, we must learn.

If you are going to be a good trainer of dogs you will need to look at your attitude toward them as carefully as you look at the dogs themselves.

What I did not tell my farmer friend was that every night when I say my prayers I ask God if he will allow me to live just a little longer than my last dog. If I am going to rely on my prayer being answered then I must try to play fairly and not keep adding dogs – it might appear that I'm trying to live forever.

Would I do a thing like that?

I would if I could.

Chapter Two

Beagle or Bagel?

If we insist only on our own analysis of a situation we will get nowhere, but if we can step outside ourselves and try to imagine the dog's observation of what is going on we will make more progress.

I believe that the biggest problem we have when trying to train dogs is that we see things too much from the human point of view.

I do not expect to get the dog's view absolutely right every time but I'm sure that attempting to see it from their angle adds a much greater degree of understanding and we are, therefore, much more likely to come closer to what is really happening.

My daughter Helen, her husband Bill and our grand-daughter Kirsty joined our whole family for Christmas here at our home in South Wales. I single them out because they brought with them Helen's new puppy to join our fourteen dogs.

Why have I got fourteen dogs?

For a little over twenty years I have earned my living training sheepdogs to a level where demonstrations of their skills have been sufficiently popular for me to be profitably employed. I have also trained a lot of other breeds but more of that later. For now, let's deal with puppy Binky.

Binky is a beagle (or, by my daughter's little American niece Rena's definition, a bagel). Beagles are scenthounds and that description should provide more than just a hint as to what motivates this particular breed.

There was, of course, the 'will it be all right if—' telephone conversation beforehand, plus, of course, reassurances about the standards of good doggy behaviour already achieved. Anyway, we all agreed that to bring Binky would be acceptable, a good idea even. The conversation ended with a unanimous 'yes' plus an observation from me that I could always house the puppy in our kennels should she prove too difficult to keep indoors.

Daughter and family arrived bang on time complete with a 'nose on legs', a very neat sleeping basket and a pile of warm blankets. Binky ran around the kitchen to explore this new and very exciting place, made even more exciting to her by the fact that Ben (a now retired Welsh Border collie) lives indoors.

Ben has reached the age when a basket full of blankets is more exciting than a basket full of female. The dogs took just a few minutes to settle in to this new situation, as though similar meetings happened all the time. The humans, inevitably, had made endless mental notes about how they would handle the event and talked knowingly about tactics and strategies; but the dogs just got on with it.

I noted a fascinating comparison: the dogs took twenty minutes to settle down, the humans were still talking about it four hours later.

What's in a Name?

Here is an interesting point and one that should help to shape the way we train our dogs. Welsh Border collie, beagle, cocker spaniel, Labrador, puli, or pug are names we give to certain types of dog – it suits our need to categorise.

> *We can rationalise if we have a list –*
> *if we don't have one, we can't! Dogs*
> *don't need such a complicated*
> *and unnecessary procedure.*

Dogs believe the straightforward evidence of their own eyes. When one dog meets another dog each would conclude, 'Here is a dog.' Actually, the conclusion would include one more, very important fact, 'Here is a *female* dog'

– or a *male* dog, whichever the case might be. The need to name the type is a human construct.

A springer spaniel accompanying a hunter does not make the observation that it is classically suited to the task because of its man-given name any more than a St Bernard does when it goes to someone's rescue. Rather, both find when given the opportunity (and training) that they have an extreme aptitude for the task. Only we know, or care, what they are called.

When I say I am married I don't find the need to qualify the statement by saying what type of woman my wife is. I remember my four-year-old son Michael coming back from school one day and announcing excitedly that there was a new boy in his class.

'What is he like?' we asked.

'Oh, he has red trousers,' came the considered reply.

Sometime later when we met him, we noticed immediately that my son's new friend was black. When I think back to this now, I feel glad that Michael did not find that fact worthy of mention; we adults, on the other hand, did. That could be why children and dogs make such good friends with each other – their energy is put into loving each other rather than specifying type.

When it comes to dogs, categories have been made so that we can know what sort of thing each breed is good at. Such categories also provide a kind of guarantee of the purity of a dog's breeding and an indicator toward its likely performance as well as how big it will grow, how much it will eat, and so on.

To our friend the dog, the 'type' is of no importance whatsoever. What is of importance (especially with a working dog) is to understand that your dog will be 'shaped' by its breed.

My daughter's beagle will find the lure she's drawn to investigate by her wonderfully perceptive nose much more worthy of attention than the commands Helen will call to her. However much Binky and Helen try to correct this compulsion they will not succeed completely.

Note, too, that 'compulsion' is our word for something bad whereas from the dog's point of view it is doing what comes naturally.

If the training is not tailored to the tendencies of the breed little or no progress will be made.

Binky's magnet will always be the wonderful stories her nose is telling her. She will spend much of her exercise time on a lead because given the choice between fascinating smells and staying close to her mistress she will nearly always chose the former.

A human has an unimpressive five million scent receptors – just two per cent of those owned by the beagle – which is why a sniffer dog can find an ounce of cannabis in a ton of luggage while we could not detect it in one closed suitcase.

Quite a difference in capability!

The breed describes behaviour. It is with dogs as it is with people. I can manage anything that uses intuition or creativity but fall apart very quickly if faced with a column of numbers. Both my aptitude and ineptitude are 'dyed in' to me. So, if you have a Labrador, a setter, a poodle, a pug, or any other named breed, do some reading to find out how the task that your type of dog was bred for will affect the way they behave.

Get to Know the Dog You're Dealing With

In most cases 'compulsion' would be a more accurate word than behaviour.

Herding dogs will round up your family and will not be shy about giving your ankle a small nip if you are not doing what you are told. They will also have a tendency to be restless; their brains will be as much in need of food as their bodies. If you do not give them enough exercise, both mental and physical, they will provide their own stimulation by perhaps working out how many minutes it will take to eat your sofa.

The choice of dog is all important, more important than I can sum up here. The big mistake, or the great satisfaction, will live with you for the next decade plus.

So, with a named breed you can read all about it but what about the dog that doesn't run true to type? What about the dog that is of uncertain ancestry? What about the dog that has suffered some sort of trauma in its early life that disturbs normal behaviour . . . the nervous dog? What about the dog that was removed too early from its mother and did not have time to learn its doggy lessons?

What about the rescue dog that comes with no kind of history and even age and breed are uncertain?

I will show you how to look at your dog (breed known or unknown) in a much more discerning way.

I have written this book in such a way that it will be useful to anyone who has a dog – notice the simplified description – whether it be rehomed, rescued or obtained in the time-honoured tradition of buying a puppy. And what I set out to cover leans heavily toward the sensitive dog, the difficult dog, the dog that has some kind of obstacle preventing successful communication.

To this end, I have looked at other people's dogs, especially rescue dogs, and made helpful observations from which all dog owners may benefit. In addition, in later chapters I document the training of my two 'candidates' Ceri and Jack – both of whom have built-in obstacles to anything that looks like training. This account of the dogs' progress is set within a time-frame so that you might have a clear indication of how much time needs to be invested as well as how you need to adapt your method to suit the dog you are training. You will find, also, a range of case histories encompassing various breeds of dog and a host of problems.

Binky's Christmas Celebration

Our doggy visitor was settled in a large conservatory which joins on to the kitchen. Ben slept there with her.

What did Binky do overnight in a strange house?

During the long night she overturned and broke several plant pots, ate a whole packet of Christmas chocolates (including the silver wrappings), demolished a generous portion of Christmas cake and wet the floor several times. In the morning I found a largish quantity of potting compost and broken plant pots together with scraps of silver foil and a puppy with a very fat stomach.

Why did Binky do it?

The conservatory has a wide, stone, internal window ledge running along two sides of it. Helpfully placed is a large arm-chair to serve as a puppy step from floor to ledge. The ledge directly overlooks a wood which comes up almost to the conservatory windows.

In the wood there are foxes, rabbits, hedgehogs, mice and voles and, to add to this, farm cats will walk down the path alongside the window. A host of most tempting scents!

The puppy is asleep in a kind of rural version of Piccadilly Circus. The air comes through the tiny gaps between the window frames and works like a magnet on the nose of baby Binky – humans would merely notice it as a draught but dogs (especially a beagle) can instantly analyse each individual wonderful scent. In addition, there is that panoramic view of the woods. Wanting to get closer she clambers up via the armchair and walks around the perfectly designed window ledge puppy path knocking over the plant pots on it as she goes. En route, she discovers a packet of chocolates, obviously placed there for her enjoyment by her considerate human friends.

Bear in mind that a beagle is a scenthound – a professional nose developed especially for the task. Consider, too, that she has been placed at the epicentre of all that smells intriguing and attractive and that chocolates have been left as an extra encouragement. The wet floor? Well, hard work like that makes a dog thirsty and what goes in—

So what is Binky? Is she already entrapped by a host of deep-seated behavioural problems? Is she bad? No, of course she isn't! She is a puppy settled in the very worst place by humans (myself among them) who talked much but thought little.

Lesson: Think much, talk little. Try to see the scene or the situation as a dog does.

Did I manage to settle Binky into one of our kennels?
No! The kennels have an outside run. When the back door opens all the dogs dash into the run to see who is coming out from the house. Strangers (Christmas visitors) have been coming and going all day. Now, it is dusk so they can't see too well.

'Who's coming?' The dogs want to know.

'It's Dad with a strange dog!'

'This is too much. First, strangers invade the house, now they're going to take over our kennels.' The lead dog barks.

'Well, if she's barking so will I, and me, and me, and me.'

A disturbing moment has been transformed into global conflict by my lack of thought.

What should I have done? Had I taken the time and trouble to include Binky in our afternoon walk, introductions could have been made in a more subtle and gradual manner and her entry into the pack's special domain – as lodger for the night – would not have been seen by my other dogs as an unacceptable and threatening intrusion.

The detectives among you will have remembered Ben, the retired Border collie, sleeping in the conservatory with Binky. How do I know that he did not eat the chocolates? To be honest, he may have tried one, once they were on the floor. But silver foil and old teeth are not a match made in heaven. Of one thing I am sure, he would have been severely pained by baby Binky's doings.

Empathise with Your Dog

The main difficulty in our relationship with dogs is that we seldom try to see things as they do even though they try to understand our requirements. We are well and truly hung up on the concept of our own superiority. If we can manage to throw that thought away our progress as dog trainers will be rapid indeed.

Someone, foolishly, asked me what the secret of dog training is, as if there was just one, wonderful, all-revealing key to a magic lock that once opened would show us all things.

The closest observation to a single secret that I can make

is that there is a need for empathy. There is a real need to look at what did or did not happen from the dog's perspective instead of from your own.

The most progressive realisation is when you can explain why the dog did what it did and understanding replaces anger.

If you can reach this stage you are on your way to succeeding not only as a trainer of dogs but also at becoming a nicer person. Perhaps the latter is a more important point to make as 'becoming nicer' precedes being a good dog trainer: you can't be one without the other!

In the bible Jesus picks two commandments and tells us that these are the most important of them all. The second of these is, 'You shall love your neighbour as yourself.'

When I was a vicar preaching to rural congregations I would notice a look of boredom crossing the people's faces when I referred them to this. I could almost hear them thinking, 'We know, we know. Tell us something we do not know!'

It is too simple a statement to consider seriously. Most people when asking a question about either theology or dog training prefer something much more obscure, preferably something that does not have an answer or something that will not put stress on them to deliver.

My observation of this attitude is that knowing and doing are a million miles apart and that the apparently simple can be the most profound, especially when we take the trouble to do it rather than scoffing at its apparent lack of substance.

*Dog training is not for theorists
but for doers.*

Friend dog is not a sceptic but an ever hopeful and loving creature. Only man has need of commandments!

Chapter Three

The Valley of a King

The old brown ram lies half in and half out of the dappled shade of the green orchard, his fellows lie around and about, not so close as to encroach nor far away enough to indicate separateness. A woolly contentment.

I bought the ram from a farm in Shropshire after he survived an attack by dogs that had finished off the rest of his flock. He is one of a rare breed called Castlemilk Moorit. We call him Brave Heart as he, alone, fought back and held his attackers at bay until the farmer came. A sheep holding off dogs must be a rarity but if you look at his lean physique and the battering ram that is his head it is, in his case, not quite so surprising. The remains of a mobile phone that I'd kept in my back pocket during shearing bears testament to the force of his charge. Brave Heart's massive, ridged horns are employed like a bony tripod, or elbows, keeping his head off the ground as he dozes. I wonder what he dreams about? Does he count sheep? (And, are they good looking?)

There is a calmness in this group of sheep that can't be seen in commercial flocks – these ones have been with us for many years and it is as if they know that they will never go where most of their kind inevitably do. I can see that they feel secure, and that knowledge rewards me. They do not rush to browse the grass for there is an abundance of it. 'He maketh me down to lie in green pastures': experience brings the words of the twenty-third psalm to life and exposes the depth and meaning of them in a way that a vicar concentrating on the academic will never see.

This is, indeed, a most beautiful place for sheep, for dogs and for us. My words cannot describe it adequately for they are poor and cold things while this place lives and breathes. I can smell it, I can feel it both as it has been in the past and as it is now.

Imagine a giant pressing down on the land with the side of his hand and the land rising steeply out of the newly made cleft. In time, a river will run through the lowest part. This, now, is where we live: a man, a woman, a little white cat, fourteen Border collies, a flock of ducks and, of course, our sheep.

A sense of tribe and of place are important to me. It needs to be old soil so that our roots – dog and human – can be woven into the very fabric of the place. I do not believe that we are like some sort of futureless, tiny, sea anemone-like polyps building coral out of our bodies, living and dying.

Here and then gone, leaving no record other than the structure our bodies made. There is more, much more, than just that, even though it is seldom apparent to the eye.

Y Garn Fawr: Our House and Our Home

Higher up the slope of the valley, on the ridge before it dips again into the forest, where sun, shade and dapple live in fern and mossy splendour, stand the kennels. In their sunlit yards contented sheepdogs lie in dream sleep: their walk was good.

> *'Cat-flapped pussies dream of mice*
> *And sheepdogs dry and full of meat*
> *Twitch and run and sniff in sleep*
> *Come by, come by, away to me'*

It is quiet and the only voices distinctly heard have important things to say. If I spoke blackbird, house martin or jay I would pass on their news.

In the centre of all of this, seeming part of the land, as if grown organically from the earth, stands the house: large, solid and dignified. Its beams and flagstone floors whisper tales of those it owned before us – but to hear them, you have to listen carefully. How many lovers have lain beneath these ancient ceilings? How many have taken their first – and spent their last – breath in the bedrooms under the eaves? How many dogs have lived here and what were they like? How many others before me have stood exactly where I stand now, gazing down like an eagle from its eyrie toward the winding river? The river, the Usk, sparkles in the sunlight, I am lost in contentment. But we know it was not always peaceful here – arrow slots at sneaky vantage points in the house's great thick walls look down on the land.

Our house is called *Y Garn Fawr*. *Garn* means cairn and *fawr* (pronounced vower) means great so, *Y Garn Fawr* means 'the great cairn' or, in plainer language, a huge pile of stones. In the Middle Ages the house was home to Thomas, son of Iddon, King of Gwent, and it was from the house that Thomas of Garn took his name. In ancient legend – or, perhaps, in truth – and long before Thomas was a twinkle in his mother's eye, a king or chieftain was buried here and the stones piled high to mark his grave bore testimony to his greatness and his deeds. This house was likely built of those same stones.

We live in the land of no vowels, of the unpronounceable – a land and a language as old as time. Here, even the place names are like poems, or songs deserving to be sung. On still days we hear the shepherds' whistles call like lost echoes and on damp evenings the clouds, like bonfire smoke, fall lower than the hills, hills that the Welsh always refer to as mountains. Sometimes we live in a house that is on land, sometimes in one that seems to float in the sky.

In my imagination, sheepdogs in barns on distant farms tell of their adventures in the fields, hills, lanes and farmyards and each dog passes on the story to the next one further down the valley, as they have done since the first shepherds came here with their dogs. There are no house names on the gates because in this place the names don't change and in the lanes folk who look familiar are nodded to; there is solidarity and an understated seamlessness here.

All the people and all the dogs, and every bird, sheep, rabbit and cow are owned by the valley just as, temporarily, they own it.

Maureen and I came to live here in the winter of our years because something tribal called us back. Not back to where we had been before (well, not in this life) but back to where we knew we ought to be. Back to a place we belong to, a place where people know what a sheepdog is. And a place where having as many dogs as we have is not seen as some unfathomable eccentricity but the act of a right and proper mind.

Wales is the home of the sheepdog, which is why they are called Welsh Border collies, so that's where we decided to look for our home. With fourteen of them, plus a small flock of sheep and a dozen retired running ducks a normal house with close neighbours was not the perfect place to live.

We drew up a sort of shopping list of requirements: there would have to be several acres of pasture, some to be used for our sheep, and one field suitable to train the dogs in; ideally, we should be far away enough from our nearest neighbour for the odd dog barking not to be a nuisance. In a perfect world, there would be a private woodland walk so that all our dogs could rush, unrestrained, along the forest path with no danger of meeting people, other dogs or cars. To be able to never need a dog lead would be beyond our expectation. Most important of all there would be a secluded spot on which to site extensive kennels. The kennels would have electricity and central heating and would be close enough to the house for us to keep an eye on them.

Quite frankly, if we had found a house with half of these facilities I think we would have settled for it; luckily we found one with all we had hoped for, plus a few things we had not thought about.

This is where we live. Our days are full of training and exercising and feeding our dogs.

I have time to watch our dogs carefully and to learn what they are saying to me and to each other. Time to learn 'dog' thoroughly.

Our dogs, who span all of the stages of a dog's life, are all related. Bob, the greatest dog I have ever known, is now fifteen. He is, as his age would have him, a little deaf and shortsighted. He has the warmest kennel inside a stone garage. His fur is still thick and shiny and he remains handsome but I have to look after him carefully.

He does not work nowadays but does as he pleases. In his day he was clever, loyal and courageous and just now and again I spot a pale reflection of the dog he once was.

Bob made me look better than I was, doing the right thing when I had called the wrong. I owe him much. He also gave me something much more important – it is called love. Bob's love has always been steadfast and reliable.

As I get older I realise that having the best behaved dog in the world rather misses the point – what we should aim at is to have the happiest dog in the world.

When I was young I trained to be a chef, not because I wanted to but because my father believed that it would be a commercially rewarding outlet for my creativity. I gained excellent (impressive, even) qualifications but was quite useless, simply because I did not care about being a chef. I had no passion and I most certainly was not happy about doing the job. My younger brother Nigel has no qualifications in this area but cooks the most mouth-watering food. Sometimes, listening to the heart as well as the head reveals the real truth.

Dogs, like people, need to be content in what they do.

This book tells of love that is carefully aimed for there is no better fuel than love to run a dog, or a life, on.

Chapter Four

The Great Conundrum

There isn't a book in the world that can tell you exactly how a normal dog feels let alone the more disturbed rescue dog. The nearest that even the best dog trainer can get is to observe the dog's actions and, through these, try to discover its fears.

Let me state the blindingly obvious: we can't speak dog and they can't speak human. We tend to anthropomorphise, or to give a nonhuman, human characteristics. In our minds dogs think (and therefore respond) like we do.

The dog is a complex creature. Our dogs know when my car is minutes away that I am coming yet, if I stand absolutely still just twenty-four yards away from our kennels they do not know that it's me and bark as though I were a stranger. If I stand half-a-mile away in a group of people my dog sees the group but not me, but if I wave my arms it sees me.

*Dogs' eyes are designed to function
at their best when there is movement.*

If a rabbit runs past a hundred yards away my dog sees all there is to see but if the rabbit sits stock still at half the distance it will likely see nothing.

When we go out with our dog we have a very limited and local view of the world while our dog, through scent, hearing and other senses beyond our understanding, builds up a multi-faceted amalgam, or fusion, from an area miles wide. The dog's world is an enigma to us as our world is based mainly on what we see with our eyes.

*My dog understands part of my world yet
I understand almost nothing about his.*

We are so poor in our understanding that we shackle our dog on a lead – sometimes one that tightens to strangle – and if through frustration our dog nips we muzzle it. But still we have the audacity to call it our best friend. If that is how we treat our friend then may heaven help our enemies.

Dogs are not human and humans are not dogs so how do we cross this unbridgeable chasm in order to begin to understand what is going on in their minds?

My method is based on over twenty years of living with and training dogs. I put myself in their place and try to see things from their point of view. If you can succeed in this technique – see the world from the dog's, not from the human's, point of view – then the reason why the dog did what it did will make a lot more sense.

Once this stance and philosophy is embraced it is possible to make a dramatic difference and the apparently insolvable problem can be put right. Frustratingly the right place to start depends on what has happened to the dog in the past and with a rescue dog, more often than not, we simply do not know. The one thing we can all agree on is that it can be a most difficult task.

In Theory, a Bumblebee Cannot Fly

There are a lot of theorists out there but the answers to the problems of the rescue dog will only be truly understood by taking – every day – a consistent and considerate hands-on approach. The answers to such problems will not, however, be understood by just switching on the academic brain and hoping to find a theory that seems it might fit yet never being willing to put that theory to the test.

Theologians have much in common with dog behaviour theorists: both look for the complicated when the simple and glaringly obvious is staring them in the face.

Thinking about the theory benefits the thinker whereas thoughtful application benefits the dog.

If you listen to the human viewpoint, limited information will be gained but learn to see and hear what your dog is saying and the road to recovery will be much smoother to travel for you both.

I come from a background of shepherding which means to live and work every daylight hour with your dogs – and at lambing time the night hours as well. To see them and their ways every minute of every day and, through continual exposure, to learn.

When I was in Devon learning to be a shepherd I managed to get 200 of my sheep well and truly mixed up with the neighbouring farmer's – it was impossible to see which belonged to who. I tried hard to divide them hoping my dogs could sort them out but all we achieved was a total blend of two flocks. I was desperate. I was standing by the side of the field trying to puzzle out what to do when an old Land Rover puttered up and stopped next to me in the lane. An ancient, grizzled farmer wound down his window.

'Yum got they sheep mixed up with next door's,' he observed, with a twinkle in his eye.

Shamefacedly, I admitted that this was true and hoped he'd speak quietly so that no other person would hear about my foolishness.

'Yum don't know what to do, do ee?'

I confessed that I did not have a clue.

'Yer's what ee does,' he drawled. 'Put they dugs up against the hedge, yum sit on the stile and talk nicely to 'em in a quiet way.'

'What will that do?' I asked.

'Well, they sheep know your voice and they'll come to you,' said the farmer.

Then he wound up his window and, smiling like a man who knows a thing or two, drove off in a pungent cloud of diesel.

Left wondering whether this was a typical Devon farmer's joke I looked around to see if there were others hiding behind the hedge waiting for a demonstration of just how silly I was. There was no one, so, I reasoned, why not give it a try? After all, the options weren't exactly rushing to present themselves.

I called the dogs to me and sat dutifully on the stile. Then, feeling very silly and rather exposed, I started to talk to them very quietly indeed. I kept my eyes down, not willing to look up and see that the sheep had not moved and, I suspected, delaying the realisation that I had fallen for a hoax.

When I did look up I was truly amazed. My sheep had come back and were standing in close proximity to me. And the other farmer's sheep? Well, they were (unbelievably) going back home through a hole in the hedge.

My first thoughts were about the wisdom of the old countryman and how practice makes a perceptive perfect. Years later, during a university theology lecture, I noted how one-dimensional and unperceptive the lecturer's explanation was of the meaning of the line in the bible, 'The sheep know my voice.'

Theory is all well and good but it is practice that makes it valid and gives it life and colour.

Just as that old, wise countryman passed on to me his understanding of sheep, I hope I can pass on to you the benefits of my long and thorough experience of dogs so that you will see our best friend the dog in a much more understanding and useful way.

I have fourteen very demanding, workaholic dogs, twelve of which can now be described as normal. Watching fourteen dogs in pack conditions as well as individually offers great learning opportunities about the dog's world.

Sometimes, having a disturbed dog living next to a normal one aids the process of observation because I can readily compare and contrast the two. But I must be prepared for any conclusions I might draw to become confused when I see that settled dogs often produce actions or behaviour that one would have imagined to be confined to the rescue dog.

> *In a lifetime, I have had seven rescue dogs and observed many others. To say that their fears were the same would be an over-simplification but they did have things in common.*

The fear of being left was apparent in most, especially in those dogs who had lost their owners through death. Whether or not their owners had died, reluctance to regard the new human as a permanent fixture – or as being entirely trustworthy – was present in every one of these dogs in so much as they all showed signs of not being entirely at ease.

Their body language was tense rather than relaxed and in some I saw a tendency (however kind I was) to believe that the currently good situation they found themselves in could not last and things would change for the worse.

What Do We Actually *Know* about Our Friend the Dog?

In his book *How Dogs Think: Understanding the Canine Mind* scientist and professor of psychology Dr Stanley Coren writes:

There are certain things that can be agreed upon as scientific facts:

Dogs sense the world and take in information from it

Dogs learn and modify their behaviour to fit circumstances

Dogs have memories and can solve certain problems

Early experiences as a puppy can shape the behaviours of the adult

Dogs have emotions

Individual dogs seem to have distinct personalities and different breeds seem to have different temperaments

Social interactions, including play, are very important to dogs

Dogs communicate with each other and with humans

I find myself wholeheartedly agreeing with all that he says but these are cautious, scientific yardsticks not fine measurements – they don't tell us how to understand dogs but they do give concrete facts that we can hold on to.

If we think hard we can uncover some of the rescue dog's fears and maybe begin to understand the way such dogs might think. This exercise is easier for me and for the dogs I have rescued because my dogs live in a pack. This means that they are surrounded by their own kind, they share a common language and that many of their routines and rituals are established by them rather than by me.

The pack provides a much more natural existence for a dog than living as the only one of its species in a tribe of humans.

And for my dogs, the advantage of the pack is made greater by the fact that they are all Border collies – thus, a true, unmixed, natural pack.

I have also noticed how a dog that comes from a home where it was the only dog will settle much more quickly and easily than expected into its new dog pack, however extended this is and however complicated the doggy politics and dynamics are. Indeed, it will settle more quickly into a dog pack than it will settle with a new human family.

The reason, I think, is that all dogs remember being one of a litter as a puppy and thus, as adults, recognise any new pack as providers of the normal. Even though the other dogs in the pack are strangers to the newcomer, the language is instantly understood.

Imagine the dog that lives in a house where it is the only one that 'speaks dog' and where it must follow a routine and a style set by the humans, whether it likes it or not. Imagine, too, that it has already had one home that proved to be less than permanent and an association with humans who did not get the relationship right. Why then should it expect this new home and these new people to be any different from the last? Is it merely travelling to another great heartbreak? Is 'sad' the norm in the mind of the mistreated dog?

Who Needs a Hug?

How do you prove to the rescue dog that its new relationship is not heading toward the same, depressing place as before?

The human reaction is to cuddle and pet the dog, to constantly reassure it, yet the dogs I resettled into my pack received no such attention from their canine group and settled almost instantly and apparently happily.

Perhaps in the case of a newly resettled dog the cuddling is needed more by the human than it is by the dog?

With a dog that is used to you the cuddling is, I suspect, a valuable tool though grooming is probably much more useful as it is also practical and comforting to the dog.

I also note that, in the main, the dogs in my pack show no signs of recognising – or finding special – their parents or siblings, so the relationship between pack members is not like that between humans. Any demonstration of affection seems to be toward dogs they particularly like rather than close family members.

Dogs very quickly recognise the status of any dog in the group. The mother of an adult dog will chastise it while appearing not to recognise it in any special way. Females that have had puppies seem automatically to become senior in the pecking order to those that have not.

This observation might shed some light on how our dogs regard us.

When dogs greet each other they tend to sniff the other's face. I use this technique regularly and with caution born of experience. I would not recommend it to the inexperienced owner, especially with a new dog or one that still shows signs of being unsettled.

I must admit to using the sniffing technique right from the very first introduction but I am used to doing it and good at assessing the risks. It is a dangerous thing to do but I use it as a short cut to say, 'There, you know what I smell like, you can trust me as I trust you.'

The Magic Button

Described in a nutshell, my magic button technique is: hit on the thing the dog most wants to do and make that a major part of its training.

Most Border collies love work more than anything. Work is for many collies, but not all, a panacea for all mental ills.

With two of my rescue dogs the joy of working will expunge all fears and this 'magic button' can be used even before any form of reassurance begins. In fact, if I get the timing right the cure is completed very quickly.

I have taken a Border collie straight from the back of the previous owner's car and, with no settling-in period, worked it on herding sheep. The joy of doing this job overpowered any fears, worries or suspicions the dog might have had and virtually resettled it in one fast move. This suggests to me that the dog has made a favourable comparison between its old, boring – maybe even deeply frustrating – existence and its new, much more exciting working life and, in addition, can identify me as the source of this much improved version.

Interestingly, in this situation the dog seems to make no judgement on how long this new, good situation might last and there appears to be no lingering suspicion in its mind that things might change back for the worse. I suspect dogs remember and worry about the past but waste no effort on worrying about the future.

A Strong Sense of the Here and Now

We humans judge the world by what we see, read and hear. We tend to like to know who did what, where they were when they did it and why they did it, as well as what it might lead to. Many of us worry about things we cannot change and can have no effect on. We are inclined to worry needlessly.

Dogs are more realistic – they concern themselves with the

here and now, and perhaps a little of what happened before in so much as it might shape or influence the present. They are concerned with their immediate world as they see it.

Dogs do not gather their information in the same way that we do. When we lived as hunter gatherers and possessed sharper senses, we probably saw the world much as they do but now our judgements and perceptions of it are based on more remote information. For example, if we want to know about tomorrow's weather we can watch the forecast on television or look it up on the internet, instead of looking up into the sky and judging for ourselves. A dog, on the other hand, 'feels' its world with all its well-developed senses.

I remember realising, much to my surprise, how close to the surface my primitive senses were when I was studying woodland wildlife and spent nights out in a cold forest. The veneer of civilisation is very thin and just underneath the surface are instincts that I would not have thought modern man still had. The eyes seem to grow larger to make the best of poor light, the ears listen more acutely for the smallest sound and the nose detects scents efficiently. The step back to regain this aspect of our past can be made more easily than I would have imagined.

The dog, however, has never lost these skills. Because of its superior hearing and scenting ability – and the other senses it possesses, the ones we cannot imagine – a dog will know that a thunderstorm and heavy rain are coming long before we do. It will know that the occupant of the car that is approaching is its master or mistress. Dogs will sense an earthquake before it happens – as will other animals and birds – while we remain unaware of it until we feel the first shocks.

Watch a room full of people and you can see (and time if you want to) information being passed around, even if you cannot hear the words. In my pack I have not noticed the dogs passing information from one to the other and it seems that each dog makes its own, instant judgement and arrives at the same conclusion. There is no delay, they all seem to know the same thing at the same time and, unlike ours, their news gathering is not distorted by bias or inaccuracy or lack of careful listening: I believe that each dog receives the same true information and that this is not changed by 'personal' interpretation.

If I am in a bad mood, or tense, or fed up they will all know immediately, almost as if they have some doggy broadband that each can tap into, and each dog will gather the same, up-to-date information at exactly the same time.

The Training 'Game'

So, how does the dog trainer tap into the canine communication network? How do we let our dogs know what we want them to do, and how do we understand what they want of us?

We have to shift our mindset and try to enter the world of the dog.

The dog is still a hunter and thinks like one.

To the dog, 'play' is all important. Our understanding of play is time off to relax, to waste time, to be non-productive but for dogs, playing is the glue of their existence.

Play exercises social interaction. Play tells each dog where it fits in the hierarchy of the pack (be that canine or human) in order that the pack's survival chances are enhanced. Running strengthens the muscles and tunes up the hunting skills. Every sniff gives the dog information about who and what passed by, their state of health, the direction they were taking and, importantly, where they might live and whether they are dangerous or not.

Dogs do not say to themselves, 'I really must get back to work as I have wasted too much time already' because play is work. Play is an essential part of being a dog.

*Dogs like play and **need** it.*

So when you are training a dog, especially a rescue dog or any nervous dog, give a huge helping of what it wants before asking it to do what you want. If the exchange rate is fair it will actually speed progress.

One of the things a dog judges your mood by is your voice or, perhaps more importantly, the body position that you assume before delivering a particular volume or tone of voice.

As an example, you cannot shout an angry 'SHUT UP' without tensing your muscles top to toe and changing your facial expression. Try it, and you'll see what I mean. Conversely, if you say, 'I love you' your shoulders come down and your whole body relaxes. A person about to inflict violence changes the way they move and their posture completely – shoulders are hunched and forward, jaw is stuck out, eyes are narrowed.

Your dog watches body shape first and uses the tone of the voice as confirmation.

We would do it the other way round.

So, if you say sweet words to your dog but these are not backed up by fitting body language your dog will know instantly that you do not mean them. Equally, a dog being told to get off the sofa will not take much notice if your body language is saying the opposite.

A dog reads body language more easily than you read the words in this book. Every dog is light-years ahead of you in its ability to read and understand what you really mean.

When you are training a nervous dog avoid changes in body language by being calm and relaxed. Do not make sudden movements especially those that raise the arm and the hand. Do not hunch your shoulders and with a newly, rescued dog avoid staring into its eyes.

The Importance of Body Language

- Do be careful not to send the wrong body language signals.
- Narrowed eyes are telling your dog to beware.
- If you lean too much toward your dog or loom over it you are signalling aggression.
- Hunching the shoulders or pushing the head and neck forward suggests attack mode.

> • Stand up straight and keep your distance, at least until your dog feels confident that your intentions are kindly.

I notice with a couple of my more nervous dogs that any physical contact that is too firm or too prolonged makes them anxious, whereas a pat, or repeated pats or touches, is seen as part of a game. A firm hold is seen as a very dangerous threat.

To pick it up off the ground (albeit in satisfaction at a good move) is, to the dog, a blunt and physical demonstration of your ability to overcome it and dominate by physical strength – the same applies to pushing a dog down.

So, to reiterate, make the training like a game: in the dog's mind this will make it far more important and relevant than something that looks like serious work. A dog can sense the degree of your intent and will be very much put off if it is too intense. If the dog likes running for a ball then play the game and use the ball to your advantage.

Do you see what I mean about the need to shift our mindset?

Work is pointless and frightening. Play is real and useful.

Let me make this clear. Anything that feels like play is good. Anything that looks like determined human resolve will hamper progress.

How will the dog know which is which? Your body language will tell it, so remember: body language and voice need to be synchronised.

In later chapters you will see how this applies in practice as I train one rescue dog and one very nervous dog. As I explained in chapter two, I shall give a move-by-move account and be candid and straightforward about the success or otherwise of every single stage of my two candidates' progress.

Chapter Five

Chapter Five

Can You Really Be the Pack Boss?

A lot of training manuals dwell on the importance of being the pack boss. In my view, this is over-blunt and myopic nonsense. There is a tendency to dumb down anything that is difficult to achieve with a catchphrase which when examined turns out to be without value.

I have used the words 'pack boss' because I needed to find a simple and all-embracing expression but, taken at face value, the words imply that the process is much easier than it actually is.

How can you be pack boss if you are not a dog?

How can you be pack boss if you do not understand the dynamics of the dog's world?

How can you possibly become pack boss when you can't even speak dog language?

Was there ever a dog that couldn't tell the difference between a human and itself?

The answer is, no, we cannot become the pack boss. But what we can do is to become a friend with authority.

> *We can be just a little like an alpha dog but without the mean streak necessary to that role.*

An alpha dog is the leader of a pack because it is bigger and stronger than the others and ruthlessly prepared to prove it, whether convenient or inconvenient. Proving its superiority at every opportunity is all important – and imprinted in its genes. An alpha dog cannot avoid doing it (a bit like some humans).

It is first to the food and believes that it owns the breeding right to any female dog it meets. For the sake of its own survival, and the discipline of the pack, it will ruthlessly squash any challenge as quickly and as effectively as it can.

An alpha dog is supremely confident, not because of its power to reason but because its genetic makeup has bestowed upon it greater physical strength and mental ability than its fellows. An alpha dog also has a more than generous ration, or overdose, of that high-octane fuel called testosterone – and the dog cannot resist its drive.

Alpha is the first letter of the Greek alphabet, in other words the most important: an alpha dog takes being first as its right.

As you already know, my pack of dogs is a large one so I have the unique opportunity to study how a pack operates. Watching my pack not only tells me quickly who the canine boss is, but also gives me a lot of clues as to what sort of glue sticks any pack together.

When I do a demonstration with seven or eight dogs working at the same time the pack boss is more often than not a female but, when the dogs return to their kennels, a male takes over the pack's social management.

You could argue that during a demonstration where the dogs do what I have determined, I am the boss. I do not see it that way: I simply orchestrate, provide the overall picture because of a particular skill, but they execute all of the movements. My role is temporary and I am used by the dogs as much as I use them.

Under these circumstances they find me functionally useful in much the same way as a dog with a greater scenting ability would be used by the pack to lead that particular activity. Once this job was achieved the scenting dog would return to the ranks. This kind of use of special skills suggests to me that the dog's world is a rather more sophisticated and complex place than we imagine.

Pack leaders seem to be born to the role but will not assume it until they are at the peak of their physical and mental powers.

Because the prime of a dog's life is short compared to that of a human, the pack boss situation is fluid. While in its full flush there is no argument about who the alpha dog is but as age robs the dog of the powers that made it dominant the hierarchy changes, sometimes peacefully and sometimes not. Sometimes, the former alpha dog seems unable, or finds it difficult, to adjust to the lower ranking that age determines for it.

A little like people then?

Do Dogs Talent-spot?

When Susie came back to us at a year old, having been rescued from an unsuitable home where she'd been deemed too much of a handful, I could see how much she needed to work, so she was introduced to the demonstration team within two days of her arrival. The other dogs were much more skilled than she was, as well as being bigger, stronger and faster, and thus they ranked higher in the tribe.

For three years, without showing any signs of lack of confidence, Susie worked on the fringe of the pack while the more important dogs occupied the centre. She worked brilliantly which sent a message to me about her potential and, perhaps, to the other dogs as well. She, not I, chose her position on the fringe and any amount of encouragement from me could not change it until she herself felt ready. I would have liked her to come into a lead position earlier but she insisted that this would not happen until she decided it was time.

As she became more important in the pack Susie worked her way closer to the centre of the action until, eventually, she moved next to the dog leading the formation. For the last two years she has imperiously commanded the centre position and all the other dogs follow her lead.

Does this mean that the dogs recognise talent?

I think it does. Working in a demonstration group is my dogs' equivalent to hunting and, to be successful at that, recognising individual talent would benefit the whole pack.

The big question here must be: do the dogs deduce this by a process of reasoning or is it an automatic part of their survival needs?

There was no evident struggle between Susie and the other members of the pack, she simply graduated to the lead position and the dogs who had previously commanded the demonstration group peacefully allowed her to take control.

Interestingly, when they go back to the kennels after the demonstration Susie reverts from leader to being a pack member and it's Gemma who is in charge. The reason for that is that she was mated with the most powerful alpha dog and many of the dogs in the show are actually her sons and daughters. On top of this, I have used Gemma for years as my wise right hand and this special relationship pushes her higher up the ranking.

There's More than One Boss

Interestingly the biggest and strongest dog in my pack is Barney yet his influence seems confined to breaking up fights between other pack members. While saying this, I note that Barney has not been mated with any of our females so his position in the pack is diminished by his lack of offspring. Jack, Ceri and Muppet are not 'whole' dogs so their ranking is lower but I would have to look very hard to notice because the difference is a subtle one.

So, according to every dog expert there is in every dog pack, wild or domesticated, both an alpha male and an alpha female, as well as beta dogs who are lower in the pack order.

I think that it is much more complicated than that.

I believe, because of my unique opportunity of being able to watch a pack in operation every day, that there are functional or 'task' pack bosses as well as an overall 'governor'.

Sally, who does not work at all (in my human judgement), hears the rustles and squeaks of small rodents in the grass better than any of the others so she takes the dominant role in this hunting area, just as Susie takes the lead for show demonstrations and Gemma dominates in the kennel area.

So, if it is all as complicated as I suggest here, how on earth are you going to send a human message to a dog to tell them that you are the boss? And, as an aside – but an important one – are you the natural boss in your human household?

The truth is that human households don't have pack bosses for all areas but use the special gifts of the members on a shifting basis.

Let's take a look at this human pack that friend dog has to live peacefully with. In physical terms its structure is a little like that of the dog pack: there will be a biggest and strongest one and, in most cases, there will also be a slightly smaller one, and there just might be one or two much smaller ones. The dog will instantly recognise the real status of each even if you are not prepared to acknowledge it. I suspect, too, that the dog recognises the special talents of each of the household's members but in dog terms.

To the dog, the basic structure is not so different to its own family in so much as the adults will be the authority figures and the children will be the puppies. The biggest and the strongest will be recognised, as will the cleverest, and the dog will 'try it on' (or not) according to where it sees itself in this slightly familiar but nevertheless foreign structure.

It is better if one person in the family trains the dog. Dogs, like people, cannot cope as well with two masters.

A human family should notice which one of its members has the most success with the dog and, more importantly, which human the dog chooses. Then, in order to make sure that the dog receives consistent training, the others should fall in behind this person.

I would not, however, let a young child train a dog even if the dog appears to choose them. The dog will most likely have chosen the child because they play more and, as you want work to *look* like play, but still *be* work, you will be able to appreciate why I say this.

Dogs have more intelligence than we credit them with and they know that we are a different species to them. However, dogs will quickly understand the right messages providing we try to understand how to deliver them in such a way as to motivate the dog to learn.

A Gentle Authority

Whoever trains the dog needs to become the source of interest and excitement for the dog. The person who gives it food, the person who gives it exercise, the person who grooms it will always establish a rapport quicker than anyone else. The provider of these needs will always be closer to the dog and the dog will always be closer to them: it is in the human family's interest that this is so. In our household, I deliver all of these things but my wife and I attend together to the important matter of food.

Signals to your dog such as voice, hand or whistle must always be the same whoever delivers them. Right down to the choice of word used.

It will hamper a dog's training if one person says 'sit' and the other says 'stop'. Everyone must use exactly the same instructions!

How long would it take you to learn if the roles were reversed and you kept getting one bark from one dog and then an irritated, different bark from the other because you were slow in understanding exactly what was required of you?

Most dogs will work out for themselves their position in the human family structure. Some dogs believe that they can dominate their human family and the way to overcome this is not by using any kind of challenging force. One demonstration that I have used with a dog that thinks it can dominate humans is the sausage treatment.

Give Your Alpha Dog the Sausage Treatment

- Cut up a sausage into slices, put the slices on a plate and spread them out so that they can be seen and scented. Take the plate to where the alpha dog is then stand next to the dog and very slowly and deliberately eat one slice of sausage after another.

- Every time the dog jumps up, add a time penalty (i.e. leave a longer interval before eating the next slice) and if he will not sit and wait, he will not get any. What usually happens is that the dog will jump up and try to steal the sausage two or three times but then, with encouragement, he will settle. Then, and only then, he gets his slice.

- If you do this three days running, the time the dog spends jumping up and down will grow progressively shorter. If he settles fast, he might get two or three slices. He will quickly realise the virtue of good behaviour and the tendency toward good behaviour, when dealing with you, will apply in everything he does.

- But do play safe: If I considered that the dog was totally unreliable I would avoid the danger and the risk of this particular exercise.

- Enthusiasm can make where fingers end and sausages begin hard to judge, especially once fingers smell of sausage – using the flat of the hand will be safest in some cases.

- *Reverse the exercise to encourage a nervous dog.* The sausage treatment exercise can also be reversed to use with a nervous rescue dog in order to achieve quicker bonding and trust. This time, use the slices as encouragement. Eat two slices before giving the lion's share to the dog but take some mouth-watering time over both eating and giving the sausage so that the gift is fully appreciated and the dog has full opportunity to see who the giver is.

Given the sausage treatment, an alpha dog will very quickly comprehend that you supply the food and will know what sort of conditions you demand from him before he gets any.

The real benefit of this is that the potentially ungovernable dog has to accept your authority over him and once that has been established the dog will understand his status in this 'pack'. The whole exercise has been totally non-violent and quick.

Experience makes me believe that the authority recognised by the dog in the sausage exercise is transferable and will make asking the dog to get off the sofa, for example, a much easier process.

Make controlled body contact

Another thing I do with both cocky and nervous dogs is to stand with the dog between my legs, making sure that it can feel a leg on each side of its body. Then I pat and fondle the dog's head and neck while still standing astride it.

For the cocky dog, this tells them gently but firmly that I am bigger and stronger than it is, but that I am still kind. For the nervous dog, the contact provides reassurance and tells it that standing close to me is a comforting thing to do.

To begin with, both types of dog might well not want you to do this to them. But start slowly, standing alongside the dog so that one of your legs touches one side of the dog's body then over a period of time, dictated by the dog's willingness, graduate to standing astride it. Avoid trying to achieve this quickly as any attempt to 'loom' over a rescue dog, be it bold or timid, will likely be seen by them as an aggressive movement.

The exercise is such a simple thing yet the benefits from it are enormous: it builds trust and bonding; it shows your relationship to the dog in a language that it can easily understand and it states your protective attitude in a way the canine mind can grasp easily.

Ignore, ignore, ignore

A good, non-violent way to stop unwanted behaviour from a

dog (alpha or beta) is to turn away and ignore them. Dog trainers call it withdrawing.

With a dog that is jumping up, snarling or growling, or just being disagreeable, looking straight at it can aggravate the situation even more. Confronting the dog by standing squarely and glaring at it is a direct and obvious challenge!

Eye to eye contact with a dog that is unsure can be seen by the dog as an aggressive and very direct confrontation and, as a rider to that, a child looking straight at the dog will be seen by the dog as a challenge it can probably win – because the dog will regard the child as a young dog that is lower in the pecking order.

*I always ignore or 'withdraw' from my dogs
in as sulky a manner as I can manage.
In other words, like any good thespian
I milk the moment for all it's worth.*

I move slowly away from my dogs and look steadfastly into the distance. I keep my hands by my sides and if one of the dogs tries to sniff or lick them I pull my hands away as though I'm seriously irritated. I do it dramatically and emphatically so that the point is clearly made. I make my ignoring routine last for at least five minutes and during this period keep absolutely silent. I do, though, make sure that my movements are slow but determined. If you pull your hands away quickly it can be misread and seen as a potential blow or an attack.

I have enough dogs for them to feel that there is safety in

numbers but this treatment always works and the message is understood by my dogs to have been clearly sent.

They try very hard to win back my affections and after five minutes – or longer if needed – I allow their requests for harmony to be accepted.

Your dog will dislike intensely being removed from your affection and will come into line quickly in order to win it back again.

Throw a mad five minutes

I must confess that during the very rare moment of real difficulty I will produce five minutes of mock madness.

What I mean by this is that I will storm around, banging and clashing everything in sight and pretending that this normally calm, gentle person has finally lost it. This will only work if whatever the dogs have done genuinely makes me angry. If I produce this 'rage' with no real feeling to back it up the dogs see through it.

Assuming I'm suitably worked up, my dogs sense that my mock madness is potentially violent and all of them react instantly. They recognise that this is not the time to aggravate the situation by continuing whatever they were doing, and so they stop. They do seem to understand what brought on my 'rage'.

If a dog is angry or annoyed it produces a growl and a stiff-legged, hackles-up token of its annoyance so that all may read its intentions – what I do is provide the same sort of warning.

A promised threat is always more menacing than a delivered one.

The glare

I do use the glare as a weapon because I know that my dogs regard me as an authority figure not to be challenged – but I still do it from a safe distance.

I direct the full stare of both my eyes into just one eye of the dog, and usually accompany this with a stiff-legged walk toward the dog – shoulders hunched forward, neck and chin thrust forward.

You would need to be absolutely sure of your status and your ground to make such an obvious demand for your dog to back down.

I urge real caution about using such a technique: its use should be rare; attempt it only if you know your dog well; use it only when you can be certain that the situation really does call for such emphatic treatment – it is risky.

Don't babble

Much of what I do with my dogs is silent as I can convey most things with appropriate body language. Dogs do not speak continually – they leave that privilege for us. I have a suspicion that dogs regard the ceaseless noise people make when they carry on a continual conversation as over-excited yapping and take little or no notice of it. That will apply to their babble of instructions as well.

Use your voice sparingly for instructions and generously for praise.

On rare occasions, be prepared to use your voice with a harsher tone: 'Get Down' to a dog sitting on the best sofa springs to mind, 'Come Back' has to be another obvious one when a dog is running perilously close to some kind of danger.

If you use a loud voice sparingly it will retain its urgency; use it all the time and it will become worse than useless as a tool. Dogs are very good at sensing the difference between the genuine and the affected: if you really mean it the dog will know your harsh tone is for real, but if you try to affect or put on a harsh tone the dog will take little notice. Dogs can spot the false quicker than people can.

Chapter Six

Spring Is Sprung

Today is different to the weeks that preceded it, in the sky a change is happening. A small war is going on between the leaden blue-black of snow clouds and the clear bouncy blue of a spring sky: they push and pull each other across the dome of the heavens disputing territory.

Inevitably (the primitive in me is not quite sure about 'inevitably') old grey winter will give way to young vibrant spring. If spring can be sensed and felt, I do both.

In the shadows it is still cold but just a yard away the sun beams down with some power, enough to suggest that my winter jacket is redundant. Not strong enough to change 'suggest' into resolve, though.

The grass – now more abundant and much more munch-able for sheep – is bathed in a more cheerful light (I wish I'd serviced my old, battered lawnmower during the winter). Drifts of daffodils stand nodding on the slopes of each rise in the ground. The trees and the climbing plants have small green buds and the sun, for the first time this year, lights up the valley from end to end.

All life, plants and creatures, waits for the last corner to be turned. Nature's suit is about to be changed. The River Usk in full tidal flood begins to take on the more cheerful blue of this new season rather than the sodden grey hue of winter. I like spring!

I am with my fourteen dogs in our training field, we are not working but wandering lazily, they from one absorbing sniff to the next and me from one engrossing thought to another. For the moment we are silent strangers, all occupied with our own matters. This book dominates my thinking and steals my attention.

My Pack

One of the many things that I like about my dogs is their ability to see that I am withdrawn because I am pondering rather than because I am offended in some way. I still watch them, out of the corner of my eye, noting their different body shapes and temperaments. They are my family, my pack, my tribe. I feel that I belong to them rather than my own kind.

Barney

How different they all are. Barney, much too big for a Border collie and almost all blue-black, just the merest smidgeon of white at his throat. 'Barns', along with his brothers and sisters, was purchased by Maureen, my wife, from a farm on Dartmoor. He comes from a long line of cattle dogs. His owner/breeder was thought to be strange because he was so soft with his dogs – a man after my own heart.

Barney's teeth lean forward as though tired and needing to find something to rest on – I sometimes wonder if he has borrowed them from someone else.

> *I notice his teeth, gums and nose are caked in mud – he is after rabbit droppings again.*

He was purchased to inject a little calm into our line but he turned out to be so laid back that we didn't breed from him. Sleeping peacefully under the shade of a tree or running to talk to the children at the theme park instead of doing his demonstration was not really the desired or expected behaviour from a working collie. We figured that if we bred from him that our dogs might turn into good-natured ramblers rather than keen working dogs.

Susie

Barns sleeps with Susie who, you'll remember, we rescued back from an unsuitable home. They are little and large in perfect harmony.

*She is a violin string stretched as far
as it will go, and she only plays the
high notes.*

Susie is a tricolour, with the brown being almost red. She's tiny (a natural size zero), wiry, busy, sharp as the sharpest thing I can think of and busy on such important business that she cannot possibly spare a single second to pass the time of day with me.

Polly
Susie's sister, Polly, I chose at the moment she was born, even before she took her first breath. Her mum, Mollie, was the original mother of my pack and I chose Polly simply because I thought that she might have inherited some of Mollie's outstanding intelligence along with the same sort of physical beauty. Polly had, indeed, inherited both these qualities and both in generous measure. Susie and Polly, so different yet from the same litter.

Muppet
Muppet stands in the distance, withdrawn, peeping around a stone wall. Old age has brought about this edge-of-the-herd behaviour. He is like an old stag, unwilling to test himself against the threat of raw strength and lunatic energy displayed by the younger dogs but always watching the hurly burly of pack life lest he miss anything. I try to involve him in the comings and goings of pack life but he has chosen the bed he wants to lie on and I must respect it.

Muppet was one of my great stars, delivering, with great

regularity, a beyond-the-possible precision in the countless demonstrations he took part in and responding instantly and always impressively to his commands spoken in Welsh.

I remember a sublime hour at the theme park when Muppet, his brother Ben and their father Bob delivered the best example of teamwork that I have ever been privileged to watch.

Their movement flowed like the very best music or poetry. They were inch perfect and as instantly responsive as fish swimming within a shoal. If I never see such a beautiful thing again I shall not feel cheated.

But wouldn't you know it? This truly great display happened during a practice session between shows, so only a couple of bystanders would have seen it. I only hope they realised the sheer quality of what they witnessed.

Muppet, a subtle, clever, stylish, leggy tricolour – beautifully marked on his legs with a freckle-like dapple that reminds me of a thrush's chest. He, too, is a rescue dog. I sold him to a farmer who, because he reckoned he was untrainable, chained him up under a tractor in a barn. What the object of such unkind treatment was is beyond me, so it was certainly beyond poor Muppet's understanding. Out of sight out of mind perhaps. How wrong that farmer was . . . in several directions!

Jumping instantly at the chance to take Muppet back, we left our warm dinners uneaten on the table and headed to the farm, there and then. We drove like (as they say in Devon) 'hell's bells' or, as the rest of the world would say, 'with all possible haste'.

I can remember Muppet's obvious delight when we put him between us on the bench seat of the van to bring him home – he took turns leaning affectionately, first on Maureen, and then on me. Collies like a good lean. He seemed to know that this was for keeps and showed no anxiety about returning to his past life, neither did he worry about its permanency, or otherwise. It was a great and lasting moment for us as seldom in life is there the opportunity to put mistakes right.

There was clear evidence of Muppet's absolute pleasure when, arriving home, he was put into a cob barn (known in Devon as a *shippen*) with warm, sun-kissed walls four feet thick and with a bed at least three feet deep in that year's golden corn straw – imagine just how nice that smelt! The barn's thick walls meant that inside was quiet, warm and sheltered from the weather but also satisfyingly immersed in it.

Even now, Muppet often sleeps outside his kennel choosing, instead, to settle down between bales of sweet meadow hay under the protection of a lean-to roof. My torch beam picks out the top of his head above the hay when I go to shut the kennels up for the night. The hay looks so comfortable that I am tempted to join him.

Ben

Ben, as I said before, is Muppet's brother; he's also tricolour, but stockier. He is now a dignified old boy who neither hears nor sees too well. He lives indoors, sleeping on a tartan travelling rug with his back against the Aga, or Misty (who you'll meet in a moment) or, in winter, both.

He has earned his rest after working for years in an understated, dependable way; always gentle with very small lambs – and with all other creatures, great and small. I do not think that he is robust enough to put up with the hurly burly of a dog pack.

Misty

Misty lives indoors, in Aga country, with her soulmate, Ben. Misty (of the surgically enhanced hip) moves with an ungainly gait, keeping an ever-watchful eye on Ben, guiding him through his dimly seen world and keeping him safe from all danger.

> *I notice how Ben looks for her, how dependent he is on her keen sight.*

Misty is soft and fluffy, a shampoo and conditioner advertisement hiding a very aware dog who, because she cannot run as well as the others, has developed the knack of always being in exactly the right place at the right time – a lesson in how to herd sheep by employing brain rather than brawn.

Bob

I spoke of Bob at the beginning of this book. Bob is the daddy of them all. Now fifteen years old, he walks stiffly, gingerly even, carefully keeping away from the younger dogs – those irresponsible teenagers who dash past him in their daily I-am-a-sheepdog game.

He has a dark, mysterious, expressive face.

In his heyday, Bob was the maestro –
absolute master of his art. I shall never
see another with such gifts.

Now, as you know, Bob lives in the end kennel against the wall, the kennel bathed in the soft, infrared glow of a lamb heater. I cosset him, ensure his comfort. Shepherds are in debt to certain of their dogs and I know that I owe this dear old boy a great deal. In my mind's eye I see him moving swiftly across the Devon fields . . . Then think how cruel that time must move on.

Sally

A hysterectomy has added bulk to Sally's small frame. She does not run but prefers to lean on my leg and 'talk' using soft sounds. Sally likes work about as much as I like income tax.

My daughter Helen, a natural-born storyteller, imagines that Sally would like us to sit upon stools, gathered in a circle, ready to hear her life story. Then, Helen says, Sally would ask us, 'How long have you got?' We would settle down and Sally would tell her tale.

'I have not had an easy life, you know. I was a single mother when I brought up Ceri, put him through sheepdog college, you know . . .'

And so Helen's Sally story goes on – it always makes the humans laugh. I suspect that Sally would have that soft, Devon accent that I love so well.

Khuni

Sally's sister Khuni – who, as I watch her now, has just found the most exciting sniff – is quite different to her sibling. Khuni's creator made her the wrong way around – where black ought to be, she has white. The black is confined to small patches around each eye, which makes her look like a raccoon, hence her name.

Khuni is another continual movement machine but slower now than she used to be. She is also an observer, liking to sit on a grassy ridge and watch the animals and people go by along the valley road below, and to warn me of their presence with a bark.

Gemma

I have already introduced you to Gemma, one of my older dogs and the mother figure in our pack – though not the actual mother of all our dogs. My wife calls her BF which stands for Baby Favourite. The reason for this is, I think, because Gemma is always where I am, stuck to my feet. Perhaps it is I who should be called BF? I, after all, am the focus of Gemma's attentions.

Gemma is calm, and wise, and acts as though she understands all things.

I always get the feeling that she owns a secret cache of intelligence which is hidden from the eyes of mere humans. She does not consider herself a dog but, rather, a shepherd. I secretly imagine her gathering the other dogs around her in their yards at dusk so that she can share her wisdom and insight.

Megan

Megan is smooth-coated, broad of head and powerful. Even when she is in season no suitor dare approach, no doggy blandishment impresses Megan. She is strong and smooth running, gobbling up ground like a silkily oiled machine. Underneath all that show, however, lies a pretty nervous dog – albeit a very single-minded one.

Fadey

Last, among the 'normal' dogs (though normal is a bad description for this one) is Fadey. We chose this name because the brown parts of her fur remind us of the colour of old, faded tights!

> *Fadey seldom seems to listen to any spoken command yet she achieves wonderful results every single time.*

I tried to do a dog demonstration without her just once and the whole thing fell apart because she was not there to set the distance for the other dogs to work to.

Fadey is an eccentric destined, I suspect, to be so because of her genes. I could quite easily have included her among those dogs that need special training but her eccentricity has served me well and, more importantly, beneath the grumpy facade she presents to the doggy world, she is a happy dog.

What Is a Rescue Dog?

I have yet to describe two of my dogs. Soon, I will reveal their names and the reasons they are set apart from the others. But first, let us consider what a rescue dog is.

The most obvious example would be the dog that, for whatever reason, has had another home before it came to live with you.

Often there is some sort of trauma involved, ranging from the unsettling disturbance of rejection to real suffering. The great difficulty is that there is usually no record of what has, or has not, happened to the dog. We can only guess. There is no history.

It is safe to say that in most cases the relationship between the first human and the dog was less than perfect, which is why it has been moved on.

It is worth noting, too, that even if you do get some sort of information about your rescue dog this is not guaranteed to be absolutely reliable. If the dog could give an account I would listen more attentively to that, and trust what it told me.

Humans get hearsay mixed up with the reality, or misinterpret what they see, or maybe even add colour to suit their own bias. Indeed, you may simply be denied important information. For example, not all breeders would admit that the mating that produced a malfunctioning dog was an accidental one – between brother and sister, perhaps – and that there might therefore be a genetic reason for this dog behaving strangely. Whatever the real truth of the matter, more often than not the dog is presented as the villain of the piece.

If the dog is being passed over to you directly from its previous owner, then take what they say with a pinch of salt. Not too many people will confess to what has really happened, especially when it comes to the frank reporting of how they have treated the dog. If I appear cynical, the reason is that long experience has taught me to be. When I was a vicar preaching to a congregation it was interesting to notice that when I was describing human failings, each person obviously thought that I must be looking at the person next to them.

There can, of course, be a host of different reasons for a dog to be rehomed. The behaviour of the dog might offer some clues as to whatever the situation might have been but we can never know exactly what took place.

My view, always, is to see what story the dog's body language tells and decide for myself if that contradicts any human version of events I might hear.

As I said before, if I had to choose between the human's or the dog's story, I would always believe the latter.

Defining the Ear-to-Mouth Obstruction

I must confess that I find the word 'rescue' limiting – it is too narrow a term, too confining to describe what I am talking about here.

A breeder, for example, might apply the term 'rescue' to a dog they take back, having sold it as a puppy which turned out not to be truly wanted by the new owner. It is only too easy to fall deeply in love with a dear little puppy that smells of milk and biscuits but, for the fickle owner, it is almost as effortless to fall out of love with the unresponsive, leggy, naughty 'teenager' – demanding much work and time – that the puppy grows into.

Breeders can only judge the suitability of potential owners by what they say during what is often a very short meeting. When I bred dogs I used to be thorough in 'interviews' with people who wanted to buy a puppy from me. I'd listen to what the prospective buyer had to say and watch how they acted, then attempt to match human to dog – in some cases I'd simply say, 'No.'

Even then, I still got it wrong a few times and have three of the returned 'mistakes' – Susie and Muppet among them – still living with me.

The word 'rescue' is too much of a catch-all, not anywhere near elastic enough, so let me add a few more to broaden the scope and embrace what I am looking at here: save; free; set free; liberate; release; salvage. I shall deal with each of these variations in later chapters.

Essentially, I am talking about the nervous, stubborn, unwilling, frightened or even apparently deaf dog that does not want to be involved with any kind of training.

In other words, a dog that has an obstruction between *its* ear and *your* mouth – be that physical or, much more likely, psychological. A dog that appears not to hear you or, worse, one that did hear you but stubbornly resists any communication you utter.

It could be a newly rescued dog or a dog that has lived with you for some time – don't worry, I shall clear up the ambiguity in this statement . . .

Chapter Seven

My Candidates:
The 'Imperfect' Perfects

Now, as promised earlier, I can reveal to you the first of my two dogs 'set apart from the others': Ceri.

Ceri – pronounced 'Kerry' – looks a lot like my first rescue dog, Annie, who now lies buried on the ridge overlooking our old shepherd's cottage in Devon (I tell her story in my first book *The Dog Whisperer*). Ceri is the only one of my fourteen Border collies that has constantly pricked ears, like Annie, and, again like her, he has a fine, lustrous coat that billows in the slightest breeze.

Ceri, too, is a rescue dog but not in the same sense as

Annie: I found her on the road! Ceri was bred by us, by accident: Sally sneakily fluttered her eyelashes at Bob and nature and a hormone overload saw to the rest. Fortunately an excellent pairing if not an intentional one.

For quite some time I could not understand why Sally looked triangular when she sat down and, rather naively for a dog breeder of some experience, was surprised when Maureen suggested pregnancy as the possible reason. I had seen no evidence of her being in season but Sherlock Holmes Bob had needed a far less obvious clue. 'Absolutely impossible,' I told Maureen. How wrong can you be?

All of Bob and Sally's puppies were sold but, unfortunately, Ceri's new owner was less keen on him than he'd thought and after six months asked if we would take him back, threatening the dog's ultimate end as an alternative.

I suspect that Ceri, true to the Border collie breed, had too much spirit. People who do not understand usually misinterpret spirit as bad behaviour rather than as a pointer to great ability. A working sheepdog puppy should sit right on the line that divides being a real handful from being as mad as a March hare. A spirited handful can be softened, the spirit channelled to produce brilliance. On the other hand, absolute lack of interest is much more difficult to work with.

Ceri's owner had pointed to all sorts of difficulties that were, according to him, beyond cure. Not one, of course, caused by him.

As I said earlier, there are often inconsistencies when people tell of the relationship between them and their dogs that ring no bells of truth in my head. The owner says one thing, the dog's body language tells a totally different tale. I tend to believe the dog.

Ceri: The Fear Inside

I don't know what had happened to Ceri but, whatever it was, when he came back to me, he was as close to ruined as he could be.

To be fair to his owner, I don't think it was a matter of physical cruelty but more a total failure to understand him. Something, though, had happened to make him cringe at a raised hand or a harsh voice – but there's no point in speculation.

> *It does not take physical cruelty to ruin a dog as intelligent as a Border collie – all it takes is an inability to understand the dog and insensitivity.*

For better or for worse, in sickness and in health, till death do us part, Ceri was back with us. He had arrived in the back of a car, imprisoned, muzzled and very unhappy indeed. There is a perceptible difference between a dog who sits comfortably at ease in the back of a car and one who has been incarcerated there. Ceri's frightened and sad brown eyes sent messages to me that I understood only too well.

His owner had had him castrated in the belief that this would soften his character. Unless it is medically necessary, castrating a working sheepdog is high treason, disloyal and a betrayal. Poor old Ceri.

Castration does soften behaviour but it also robs the dog of half its reason for existing and steals away its courage. People are often too quick and too casual about taking their dog to the vet for what is in fact a drastic and irreversible operation, so please think carefully before going down this road, even if you are being strongly advised to do so. Many people now call it 'neutering', which to my mind is a neat, 'pc' way to make it sound less alarming.

The whole subject is a thorny, not to say emotional, one. The hard truth is that the vet is going to remove the testosterone factory that helps make your dog who he is. I for one do not think that cutting a bit off my best friend is a terribly considerate, loving or sensible thing to do unless, of course, there are compelling reasons for it. It's not a decision to take lightly and should only really be considered as a last resort.

> *They say that the eyes are the mirror of the soul and this is certainly true for dogs.*

Much can be understood about a dog's mental state from the expression in its eyes. I don't think that a particular gift is required to understand the general nature of such messages: all you need is compassion.

From being reluctant to take Ceri back my mood changed rapidly to one of wholehearted welcome. I managed to see the real problem, which was not the unsuitable owner who'd made me angry but the poor dog's plight – I felt such pity for him. When I see a dog as unhappy as Ceri was and know I can put all things right for it, the inconvenience, implications and consequences stand no chance at all of changing my mind.

The muzzle and choke lead Ceri was wearing were

immediately thrown away – I wanted him to know that he would never again be restrained by such instruments of torture. That made me feel better and, in a way, symbolised my resolve to cure the fears evident in his eyes.

We started, gradually, to make progress with him and bit by bit he began to look as though he might one day learn to relax: 'might' is the important word in that sentence.

While Annie, for example, was frightened of all sorts of things, Ceri's fears are more specifically related to people.

All my dogs love him to bits so, in their world, he is a nice dog. He does produce some very strange body language when they are all out together but this is more to do with him wanting the other dogs to be his friends rather than him being frightened of them. So, he is not overtly accepting that he is lower in the pecking order by capitulating but simply expressing a desire to live in peace with all. If my assessment of his body language is correct then this behaviour is most unusual indeed. Usually lower order dogs capitulate – there is no pretence or subterfuge about it, they simply do it. I sense in Ceri a very sharp intelligence and even find myself wondering if he is manipulating his doggy family just a little.

I believe the main reason he gets on with the dogs in a more relaxed way than he does with me is because he trusts them. They won't let him down; they are dogs, after all, not people.

If Ceri had a motto, I think it would be,
Never Trust a Human.

Even though I have always been kind to him – exceptionally so – his attitude seems to suggest that he expects I may not always be. Sometimes I see that wary look in his eyes that seems to say, 'Yes, you are nice to me now, but will it last?' I would say that he believes humans are incapable of consistency. In short, as far as humans are concerned, Ceri is a dog that expects bad news to be just around the next corner – because, with his previous owner, it was. This mistrust was caused, he wasn't born with it.

My Plan for Ceri

Ceri is now five years old and we have had him back with us for four and-a-half years. He is a pack animal, happiest when he is out running across fields with his canine family. He knows how to behave in canine company and has taken part in a couple of displays, and very neatly, too – but following the lead provided by the other dogs rather than listening to commands from me.

He is very much like a naughty child, refusing to toe the behavioural line until he can see some benefit for doing so, which to my mind is a pretty intelligent stance to take. He has learned, not only through my teaching but also by watching the other dogs and now, while he is, at least, more confident, all is not as it should be.

When I sniff his nose in greeting I sense two things blended together and difficult to separate: one is joy at the relationship between us, the other is reflected in the tensing of his face that prevents us bonding completely. He is certainly openly loving and more affectionate than some of our other dogs but always has an uneasy edge.

My plan is to train him, not so that he is the most accomplished dog in the world but so that he will feel at ease and confident wherever he may be.

Being able to do what I want him to do will give Ceri confidence so the working practice is important. I might use my magic button technique (which I explained in chapter four). We shall see.

Working one-to-one with me is going to be a bit daunting for him. He finds the company of his pack more reassuring, plus – and perhaps more to the point – less demanding. I think he will feel vulnerable being under close and concentrated scrutiny. Ceri has no problem living with a large pack of dogs but the same can't be said about his relationship with humans. We shall see what transpires.

I plan to be crafty and use reverse psychology to win him over. Most of all I shall be kind, patient and gentle. We shall make haste slowly – a favourite expression of mine, albeit a somewhat upside down one. What I mean by it is that success can be achieved only by progressing at whatever pace the dog's ability or willingness to learn dictates and by perfecting each task before moving on to the next.

Introducing Jack

OK, Ceri's one candidate for training. Jack, my second candidate, is my other 'set apart from the others' dog and he looks like being an even more difficult proposition.

In *The Dog Whisperer* I said, 'I have never met a dog that could not be trained once the right approach is found' – Jack will push that theory to its utmost limit. For a start, he is seven years old – way beyond the ideal age for training. I have trained older dogs before but progress has always been slower than if they'd been younger.

Border collies are meant to be black and white i.e. large areas of black, small areas of white (sometimes no white at all). Jack is white and black, a 'negative' as it were – huge expanses of white, little patches of black and his coat is curly which is also unusual.

His character? Jack's makeup is a mystery to me. Every time I think I know him he comes up with something that proves I don't. For example, he is stand-offish until that rare moment when he decides he'll be affectionate – extremely affectionate. The question is, why is he so reluctant to be wholehearted?

Shepherds are a superstitious lot and attribute qualities or faults to different types of sheepdog such as: 'a dog with a kink in his tail will have a kink in its personality' or, 'white sheepdogs are no good'. Sayings such as these don't always step up to the mark but I think the white sheepdog theory could be accurately observed – perhaps Jack's colour has some bearing on his personality and behaviour? And the kink in the tail theory? Among the dogs I have trained, the ones with a kink in the tail most certainly had matching personalities.

If I take Jack out on his own he will wander off (and I mean more Marco Polo than a meander up the lane) but he does love coming out with all the other dogs – and there's a clue to Jack's training. Jack also practises selected deafness.

He has in the past exhibited some pretty disgusting habits, too, including eating other dogs' droppings (coprophagia), and a propensity to wee on the floor (and worse) at the slightest opportunity, especially if we had laid down newspaper. Jack also, when he slept in the kitchen at our house in Shropshire, had an unusual taste for plaster, liking the flavour to such an extent that he could eat quite a large patch of wall in the course of one night. I am not talking a light hors d'oeuvre but a full four courses of the stuff. Was it the texture of the plaster in his mouth? Was something missing in his diet? An escape attempt, perhaps? I have no idea.

Jack is most adorable on the outside and pretty disgusting inside.

Jack had a difficult puppyhood. He suffered violent fits which became increasingly intense: violent spasms – eyes rolling, frothing at the mouth. I was convinced that if he continued to have them he would die. Our vet at the time – who was brilliant – suspected Jack's fits were caused by sexual frustration; I was convinced that he had a form of epilepsy.

He was given a drug that, in effect, chemically castrated him for a couple of weeks and I was told to monitor whether the number of fits he had fell. He had not so much as a hint of one and looked so much better that we knew castration could only benefit him. So, sometimes, there can be a good reason for having that particular surgery – but only once all the consequences have been thought through very carefully.

And even though he's been 'done' he's still the first to make a bee line for a bitch in season, but that is because his castration took place a long time after the testosterone was flowing and he can still remember clearly what that feels like!

It is important to note that, in the conventional sense of the word, Jack is *not* a rescue dog – he was born at the theme park where I worked as a demonstrator of sheepdog skills. He did not suffer the trauma of being sold as a puppy and has not been deprived of open spaces, freedom or attention.

However, while Jack is not a rescue dog in that narrow definition of the term, his behaviour is disturbed to such a degree that we might imagine he had experienced some similar problems. I believe that Jack's problems are not 'dyed in' but that something has *caused* them, and through observing and training I intend to find it and put it right – in other words, rescue him.

So, as well as being rescued from a different home, a dog can be rescued from

*the problems that have caused such damage
to its behaviour and its life.*

Doubtless, there is a reason for all Jack's strange behaviour but I don't know what it is. Time, however, and the inevitable closeness we will gain during training might point me to an answer.

Do I love him despite his faults? Of course I do! In fact, I have a tendency always to fall in love with the underdog, be they canine or human.

Jack's Good Place to 'Be'

Over several years we tried our very best to make life better for Jack but failed miserably.

He had been normal at our theme park home in Devon and his troubles really started at our church house in Shropshire. I think he did not like the place or, to be specific, the kitchen where he lived.

When we moved to Wales he and the other dogs suddenly found themselves in a quiet place with acres of their own land to run freely in. I think that the new-found freedom helped but, more significantly, a greater and more meaningful change was made to Jack's life, a change which proved as influential on him as the one-to-one training we are about to embark on.

Before we moved to Wales I built or, rather, assembled kennels and we shuttled the dogs around in an attempt to find their favourite sleeping places.

Each block of kennels is adjoined by a very large open

yard. Most of the other dogs quickly picked a place that suited them except Jack, who continued to treat his kennel the way he had treated his former home in the kitchen.

One day I moved Jack into an outdoor yard fringed by three kennels each of which has a sleeping area and an attached, covered run plus an ever-open door giving access to a large, gravelled, communal yard.

I had built cavity walls, ceilings and floors in each of these kennels and had stuffed the gaps in both walls and ceilings generously with the sheep's wool that comes every year with shearing. Every outside surface now had at least four inches of insulation between cold weather and occupant so cosy comfort was guaranteed. I put polycarbonate windows on the covered outside run section and a plastic strip draught excluder on each door.

Jack's bed was filled to a luxurious depth with the most fragrant meadow hay.

So, since then he has had a private, quiet space, undisturbed by the comings and goings of either canines or humans. I think this last point was the most important step for him.

Jack emerged like a swan transmuted from an ugly duckling. He no longer chewed the walls, or made urine lakes on the floor and stopped eating other dogs' faeces. His kennel is immaculate with an imprint of his body tidily pressed into the nest of his meadow-hay bed.

Jack, even then, became a much changed dog.
His personality (or dogonality) began,
at last, to shine through.

A series of coincidences perhaps? I don't think so. He did not like the kitchen at our house in Shropshire. In fact, he actively disliked it, though 'hated it' would not be too strong.

If I look for reasons I find them – but not where I would expect to.

The garage adjoined the kitchen with the two rooms divided by a breeze block wall. In the garage there was a central heating boiler standing against the dividing wall. It was controlled by a time switch and would come on once in the early morning and again in the evening and, of course, would turn off twice as well. Running down behind the plaster that Jack gnawed as a pastime was a waste pipe carrying water from upstairs so all sorts of gurgling and rushing water noises would have disturbed him at unexpected times.

Dogs are super sensitive to sounds in the
higher frequencies whereas our ears are tuned
to tones in the mid-range of human speech.

I strongly suspect that the boiler pump emitted sounds so high that we humans could not hear them but poor old Jack could and they drove him quite potty.

There may, of course, have been other reasons but, whatever, Jack did not like that place. It made him unhappy

91

and brought on a host of behavioural problems that stopped when he left it.

For Jack's sake, I wish that I had been more perceptive. Hindsight makes a wise man of me which is belated but preferable to never discovering at all.

My Mission

My task is to train Ceri and Jack and to record the rate at which we progress. We shall practise all the basics: sit, stop, walk on, come back, walking nicely both on and off the lead, and so on. I will also try to cure the bad habits they have and I will try to erase their fears. I decide to start their training routines when spring truly arrives.

Older dogs that have had difficult beginnings, like Ceri and Jack, need a far more sensitive training technique because they have fears. First, their worries must be smoothed away. Fear can completely block any progress.

I shall use my dog whispering technique throughout the training of both dogs but will aim more for contentment than compliance. Achieving both would be a bonus of considerable value.

The most important thing will be that the dogs enjoy every single minute of their training and that it stays absolutely stress free. I will only raise my voice if there is an urgent need to do so and will not even think about being irritable.

If I am successful there will be two benefits: first, both dogs will be able to respond instantly to my every command; second, both dogs will become secure in confidence and therefore much happier and far less affected by the fears that made them so difficult to train in the first place – this would be the most significant achievement.

You may be wondering why I waited so long before undertaking the formal training of Ceri and Jack. The answer is that I wanted to try to calm each without placing extra demands on them. I wanted them to feel at ease with me before starting to think about serious training.

If the dog you are going to train has only recently come to live with you and is nervous and unsure it might be wise to give it time to settle before you start the training. As I say elsewhere in this book: make haste slowly.

In this situation the tortoise will always arrive before the hare!

My Method

A word or two about the training chapters that follow: my method is intuitive rather than prescriptive. The ability and receptiveness of any dog will vary (as will the ability of its trainer) so there are no set timescales or recommended repetitions for the routines.

When I say 'keep your dog close to you', I will not give you a measurement but will leave it to you to pick a distance that both you and your dog are comfortable with. You should limit each training session to a maximum of ten minutes, but if great results are achieved in three you should not feel that the remaining seven are mandatory. Call it a day and go home happy in the knowledge that you have achieved a pleasing result.

If your dog is about to make a huge leap forward right on the ten-minute limit, take another two or three minutes so that it can complete its progress.

There are a few 'musts', though:

- You must be patient

- You must be kind

- You must be sensitive to your dog's likes and dislikes

You will notice that I repeat myself often. I have done this for emphasis, to help the learning process, and so that you do not have to keep checking back to an earlier chapter to see what was said.

Chapter Eight

Ceri and Jack:
The Training Begins

As I have said, Ceri was bred by us then sold as a puppy to a man who probably did not realise how demanding Border collies are. Ceri did not suit his new owner and his new owner certainly did not suit him – oil and water come to mind. Most people look and decide quickly on a puppy but love can drive the decision in the wrong direction. Much more sensible to read and find out about the breeds that both appeal *and* suit your lifestyle before going to look at a puppy or a dog from a rescue centre, or anywhere else for that matter. A good book on the breed would tell you that Border collies, for example, need tasks both mental and physical and they need something interesting and new to do every day.

Pick a dog that suits you because it is going to be a long partnership.

Should I Have a Dog?

It pays to take a good, close look at your own lifestyle, hobbies, personality, location and so on, before you make a decision about whether you want a dog at all or which type of dog you might be suited to.

Below are the type of questions to consider but you should compile a comprehensive list that is relevant to you:

- Are you a couch potato or an athletic, energetic six-miles-before-breakfast sort of person?
- Are you a natural authority figure or someone who'd sit on the floor so your dog can lie on the sofa? Be honest!
- Are you a 'natural' with dogs? i.e. Do you really like dogs and, more importantly, do they like you?
- Does everyone who lives in your household feel the same way about having a dog?
- Are you very house-proud?
- How many hours are you away from home each day?
- Does your job involve spending extended periods of time away from home?

- Do you have young children? How will they get on with a dog?
- Have you got a garden?
- Do you live near open countryside?

Ceri settled back in his old home with us quite easily but was obviously very unsure about people. To start with he lived indoors, but now that we live in rural sheep country he lives in a kennel, next to his pals Jack and Susie, and they share an enclosed gravel yard and a peaceful freedom not experienced by house dogs.

He has been happier outside, as lots of sheepdogs are. Ceri is the kind of dog that will lure unsuspecting strangers into a false sense of security and, when they least expect it, he can turn into a little monster. Fingers are a favourite target but he would not turn down a nibble of rump. Not a serious biter but not averse to a small, keep-your-distance nip.

Toward me he is loving and gentle and reliable, but here is a clue: I am loving and gentle and reliable to him.

April: Ceri Goes First

Today we start the one-to-one training.

My objectives are twofold

1 To make Ceri relaxed and at ease with people and that he should treat them as friends rather than chews.

2 To make Ceri excel at the job he was bred for because I believe that the satisfaction he will gain will make him relax.

First, take a good look at the dog

Today I shall look at Ceri in a totally objective way – not the usual, 'how's my pal today?' way but much more critically, as if looking at him for the first time.

I want to see what I have to work with

For a male collie he is a medium to big dog, neither too fat nor too thin. His coat is long and fine, his ears are pricked and his black and white markings are right for his breed. His face is narrow and sharp and the expression in his eyes proclaims obvious intelligence.

If anything his body movements suggest a younger animal with the kind of skittishness I would expect in a one-year-old rather than a five-year-old dog. He has been castrated – a bit like taking fast acceleration out of a racing car – yet he is leggy and still athletic.

There is a marked difference in his behaviour near sheep: his movements are more sober, steady and determined. Near other dogs he behaves like a 'teenager' and spoils every good move with a mad ending. There is a clue!

His father (Bob) was the best sheepdog I have ever seen and his mother (Sally) the least interested in anything that looks like work. So, did he inherit Bob's talent and aptitude or Sally's couldn't-care-less attitude? Or a mixture of both?

The First Session

It is April. I cannot see any joy in training in the rain with water trickling down my neck but today, for a change, the sun is shining and small puffs of cotton-wool cloud hang motionless in a very blue sky. The apple trees are covered in white blossom and many of the trees in the wood have put out tender green leaves. Yellow flowers speckle the grass.

Time for me to look and learn.

We have gone, first, to the training field, a place that Ceri is well used to but today is strange for each of us: he is the only one out here with me.

He is slightly puzzled. He asks the question with his eyes, 'Why are we out here on our own?'

If you were watching us over the fence you would wonder what on earth we were up to.

*There are no voice commands, no whistles,
no waving of hands. It is silent apart from
the songs of the birds.*

Ceri is not on a lead because this is our land and no other dog will come to join us. But, if I lived in a town and was doing this in the park, I would complete the exercise using a normal, clip-on lead.

I concentrate on changing my direction, I walk first one way then, in an over-exaggerated fashion turning – a bit like a soldier doing an about turn – and walk back to where I have come from. Using both voice and gesture, but not in too strict a way, I encourage Ceri to stay close to me. After a fashion, he follows me – but follow he does.

Next, in between walking back and forth, I stop abruptly, and each time I stop he stops too. He does it sloppily but nevertheless grasps what I am silently telling him and responds.

> *All the time I am watching. I watch,*
> *and then I watch some more.*

A couple of times I stop then crouch down on my haunches (an achievement at my age). He recognises this most friendly and universal of gestures and sits by my side.

We move away from the training field and he starts to take more interest, anything that moves attracts Ceri's attention – sheep in the field, ducks in their pen and most of all Kitty, our cat, sunning herself on a warm, stone wall.

When he spots her he drops down into that classic collie crouch and mirrors her movement by constantly adjusting his own. I allow him to walk toward Kitty and resist the temptation to call him back. I do stay alongside him in case stalk turns to rush, but it does not.

I tell him 'steady, steady' stretching the words so that they are almost onomatopoeic. He responds by slowing his progress.

Then I call him away, and on the second call he does what I want.

Rather than the word I use, it is the tone of the voice and the hand signals that indicate direction that count.

At the end of our forty-minute session – most of which is spent observing Ceri as he sniffs his way around the training field – I groom him softly, talking all the time in a quiet and reassuring voice.

Ceri has enjoyed himself immensely, his first concern about being on his own with me (which usually means work) has evaporated. He is one happy dog!

What Has Been Achieved and What Has Been Learned?

Well, I do know that Ceri is stimulated by tasks. The working dog's inheritance is his. He has taken more from Bob, his father, than his mother.

Movement spells interest for master Ceri. I also know that anything new immediately wakes him up. My voice being replayed on the hand recorder I was using fascinates him.

I have also noticed that he has an excellent brain as the tape-recorded voice did not faze him unduly; once he had seen where it came from he was content. The same thing would have driven some rescue dogs into a panic – maybe I shall use a tape recorder in future in order to study a dog's reaction to it? I have discovered that Ceri will respond to body language without voice or whistle and that he will do so much more attentively if the signals are allied to action or the movement of some creature.

A Country Dog at Heart

The truth is that the average Border collie is a country dog. Don't despair, though, if you have one and live in an urban situation. Country collies can herd sheep or ducks but town-dwelling collies have other outlets for their huge mental and physical energy, such as flyball (a high-speed ball game) and even dancing to encourage their normal alert state.

A walk around the block with your collie on the lead might suit you but it will not be the best thing for your dog. Herding dogs need to run freely and they need mental stimulation – challenges. It's time to start, at least, chucking a ball or a Frisbee. The lead has to be the most yawn-inducing and frustrating thing to a collie.

Because collies tend to get excited lots of owners seem to think that the best thing to do is to try to calm their dog down and keep it that way – like putting a genius on Prozac. A cure for your excited dog will be best achieved by lateral thinking – give them all the stimulus they need and more and this will lead to calmness through contentment.

'Calming down' by avoiding the excitement of work, or play, actually has the opposite effect and makes the dog anything but relaxed. My own dogs are calm beyond belief after a hard physical and mental workout. It is a big mistake to try and calm a working dog by offering it some sort of quiet distraction because the end product will be a frustration that makes it frantic.

Wherever you live there will almost certainly be a dog-owners' club nearby that offers obedience, agility or dancing. Join it. If you have an active dog you will not fail to miss the enjoyment on its face when it's satisfactorily occupied.

Bored dogs (especially Border collies) will invent their own exciting games if you don't provide them. Among their favourites is chasing cars, a subject that I don't need to evaluate or linger on.

Jack's Turn

As I did with Ceri, I start by taking a good, long and objective look at Jack.

The first thing I notice is that he is big, deep-bodied and sturdy. His colours, you will recall, are the wrong way around thus master Jack is a white and black Border collie. He is very handsome and has a lovely, happy expression that on closer inspection is tinged with a look of uncertainty.

A sheep farmer would not have kept him because, as I have already mentioned, there are many (sometimes irrational) theories about sheepdogs who are predominantly white. When Jack was born I vowed to hang on to him because I did not believe the shepherds' folklore and wanted, obstinately, to prove them wrong. So far, I have not managed!

As I observe Jack, his actions do not provide enough copy to fill a page – the words I gather through my observation of him are few. He is something of an enigma. I do, however, notice the clear signals that he is not motivated by work.

As we come around the corner from the training field he passes a pen full of ducking, diving, quacking, splashing

Aylesbury ducks and he does not even bother to look at them. Furthermore, when he turns the corner past the house he comes face to face with our cat Kitty who he proceeds to kiss on the end of her nose. No stalking or body tensing, no change of gait or movement.

As we walk down the path toward the country lane I try some of the same body language signals with Jack that yesterday I tried on Ceri – the sudden turning, the stopping. Because he is far too busy following some fascinating scent he does not even notice my exertions.

When I use voice signals he responds, lazily, but not totally convincingly. Unlike most Border collies he is not energised or stimulated by hints that life could get rather more exciting; in fact, he seems to look the other way as though he hopes it won't.

When we cross the cattle grid I put him on the lead. Our dog leads are used so rarely that I had to ask Maureen where we keep them and when I fished one out the leather loop at its end was stiff from lack of use.

Usually, putting a dog on a lead means that nothing useful can be observed or learned but I notice that Jack actually likes it.

I think being on the lead provides a feeling of security that he otherwise lacks. As we walk, pheasants and creatures unseen make scuffing or fluttering noises in the hedgerows and dingle (wooded valley). Jack turns his head to listen but shows no sign of any greater interest – Ceri would have been through the hedge at such temptations.

After an hour's walking with Jack and watching him, followed by a long grooming session, I pop him back in the yard with the other dogs. By the time I have walked back to the house he is stretched out in the sun, fast asleep and obviously very content indeed.

Not all Border collies are machines in perpetual movement and Jack, in fact, is quite the opposite.

I can find lots to say about his personality traits and habits but, so far, very few answers. Whatever it is that made Jack eat plaster from the kitchen walls and turn a dry floor into a lake, or why he eats other dogs' faeces, and so on is not apparent in the way he acts. Why he suddenly developed fits is answered by the vet's diagnosis of sexual frustration but, later on, when I thought about it more carefully, I wondered whether his other strange habits were the outcome of that frustration or could be attributed to his environment.

Jack, as I have explained, is not a rescue dog in the conventional sense. He has been ours since he was born so, really, we would expect him to be more like our other dogs – well-adjusted and happy. He does, however, need to be rescued from his problems.

Among my pack, fears differ from dog to dog – what will disturb one will not begin to trouble another and this is why there can be no single blueprint for how to resettle and train.

Outwardly, Jack does not appear to be a nervous dog but I know, in fact, that he is nervous. During his training period I shall continue to look at what I see in front of me as well as looking back at his previous behaviour. I will try hard to find answers – there will be some – and finding them will make all the difference to Jack's behaviour and, as a consequence, his contentment.

Chapter Nine

Anxiety and Fear

The two words, anxiety and fear, are often taken to mean the same thing; in fact most dictionaries would describe them in much the same way.

I define anxiety as worry that a particular thing (or an unknown something) *might* happen. A feeling of dread. Fear, I would describe as a feeling experienced in the presence or anticipation of physical danger of which there is prior (from a memory) or present knowledge.

As I've said, in terms of a rescue dog from an unknown home, the dog's previous life is a closed book to us. We don't know whether its parents were nervous or calm, or what the rescue dog itself has experienced but it will highly likely suffer more than a normal dog's share of anxieties and fears. And, because we will not know what makes it anxious and afraid, removing the causes will be extremely difficult.

We do know that it has suffered the disturbance and trauma of resettlement at least twice: first it has been removed from mother and siblings to a strange new home then, for whatever reason, it has been thrown out and rehomed again. In some cases this might have happened several times. I guess it must be like being serially orphaned.

It would make a good start to think about this and realise that while the dog you have rescued might look at ease on the outside, it is likely to be very vulnerable mentally.

A Sense of Place

One dictionary defines place as: 'An area, position or portion of space that somebody or something can be in.' That space, of course, can be either good or bad. Dogs thrive on stable normality: a place will be deemed normal by a dog if it stays the same.

Most rescue dogs' anxieties can be connected to place. I shall explain what I'm getting at with this example: I like going to my local pub for a drink at the bar, I enjoy being in that familiar environment. But if I were to go to my local and find the bar had vanished, my sense of order would be disturbed, I would feel unsettled! I would of course soon reason that as the publican is in the business of selling drink the bar may simply have been moved. If I were to walk into the pub and find all the furniture and fittings stuck to the ceiling, I would worry deeply at being, apparently, upside down. I would probably take some coins out of my pocket and drop them to see which way they fell, for confirmation of truth or evidence of hoax.

A dog cannot control its own space to the degree that we can, it puts up with what we give it. And the picture the deeply disturbed dog sees is probably quite close to the upside-down room in so much as things are not as they are meant to be but the dog can do nothing to change them.

> *Dogs are like people in that places need to be the same in order to be normal.*

The following anecdotes form the basis of my hypothesis regarding the importance of 'place' to dogs.

Anxiety bred of abandonment

We had a little sheltie called Gem who was very much a rescue dog. She originally belonged to an older couple who lived in sheltered housing and Gem had been their only dog. So, she had a master and a mistress and they lived all together in the same, quiet house doing much the same thing every day. A good routine had been established. It was a good 'place' to be.

After four years of Gem's settled life her master died; not in front of the little dog (which she would have understood) but in a hospital, miles away. So, one minute he was there and the next he was gone. I daresay little Gem waited for her master to return and I have no doubt that the waiting went on for a very long time. I doubt little Gem ever understood why he never came home.

Around five years later the dog's mistress had to move very suddenly into a respite home. As vicar for the village where they lived I had visited her and Gem often, so the dog knew me. I had promised the lady that if anything ever happened to her Gem could come and live with Maureen and me.

'One more dog won't make any difference to us,' I'd said.

Amid the hurly burly of her sudden move, the lady's greatest concern was, as you would expect, for her little dog. We took Gem as promised but, obviously there had been no chance to resettle her gradually. Out of the blue, Gem found herself living in a new house with new people and, again, she didn't know where the central and dearest person in her life had gone plus the routine she had been familiar with for so long had been destroyed in an instant. Gem had lost the security of her familiar place. Furthermore, she was now in a household with fourteen other dogs all bigger, stronger and faster than she was.

She adapted remarkably well to this totally different place, even though all the features, animate or inanimate, were new to her but she suffered one huge anxiety that was abiding and deep-seated.

Gem worried that the two people sharing her new life would, like the others before, vanish and not return.

A week or so after we had taken her in I had to travel to the North to do a dog demonstration and was away for four days. Maureen told me that Gem fretted continuously and

110

the welcome the dear little soul gave me on my return was one of the most feverish I have ever experienced.

Over time Gem became very attached to Maureen and the poor thing would pace the floor restlessly whenever my wife was away from home. Her worry was evident, almost tangible, and nothing would alleviate her anxiety.

Anxiety caused by change

A smaller disturbance to place can bring on anxiety. A lady belonging to the same dog internet forum as me (N4C) wrote about a chiminea that had not been used for several years because it was in the wrong place. Eventually, she and her husband had loaded it on to the back of a tractor and moved it to a new spot.

In its original position, her two dogs, Mattie and Bertie, had passed the 'fire machine' every day and treated it as part of the landscape: Bertie regularly cocked his leg against it. In its new position, however, both dogs treated the chiminea like a dangerous, invading monster and ran, stiff-legged, around it, barking and snarling fit to kill.

Now, considering that Bertie had left his scent all over it you would think he would have recognised it as a friendly fixture, but no – it was now an enemy.

The fact that the chiminea had 'moved' to another spot overpowered any reassurance Bertie must have had from its familiar smell – it was no longer something he felt at home with.

Once his owner had patted the chiminea, Bertie began to accept it again.

Animals don't see the world as we do. Hearing and smelling are much more central to their 'picture' of the world than seeing.

The good place

An old farmer friend of mine called Walter started farming before the tractor came along and therefore used horses to do the farm work; much nicer, you can talk to horses.

When he and his wife sold their first farm (where the horses were born) they loaded all their belongings on to a cart and, with their two horses pulling them, trundled some ten miles to another farm. They stayed there for nearly ten years before they discovered that they really needed more land.

This time, they were moving about fifteen miles to a new farm which was some five miles beyond their first one and on the same road. As the horses and cart approached their original farm, Walter noticed that both of them had a spring in their step, they were getting excited and as they drew level with the farm gate both (as one) turned into it.

The horses were happy because they were going, as they saw it, home. They had remembered their place after ten years of being away.

I always noted the behaviour of dogs returning to the place of their birth.

When Maureen and I ran The Sheepdog Breeding and Training Centre at the Milky Way theme park at Clovelly in North Devon, owners would bring the dogs they had purchased from us as puppies back to visit us. Most of the dogs soon recognised the place and would show signs of great joy. It would be only several minutes later before they recognised our voices.

In the case of rescue dogs – puppies who had gone from the Centre to the wrong homes then been returned – they would recognise the place fairly quickly but not until several hours later would they recognise the voices. After unhappy lives, they had been reunited with a good place, now made perfect by reassuring voices and at this point the full extent of their pleasure and excitement would be demonstrated most obviously.

It was as if the place established much-needed security and the familiar voices put the icing on the cake.

Then their greatest delight was reserved for reuniting with the canine members of their first pack who were part of this good place.

Anxiety in the Older Dog

If you add old age to the unsettled feeling experienced by a rescue or naturally nervous dog you have a compound that can change the dog's character altogether. Stiff joints make old dogs grumpy and irritable; deafness and fading sight make them uneasy; and a combination of all three (not unusual in old age) can make their world a very difficult place.

I have three dogs suffering from one or all of these problems. Fadey, who was irritable even in her prime and is now twelve years old, suffers because she cannot see which of her kennel mates is approaching and, I suspect, also cannot hear them coming as clearly as she used to. I think she feels uneasy because they seem to loom up on her with no warning.

This age-related weakness threatens her position in the pack. What could be guaranteed in her prime is now in doubt and this probably does as much damage to her confidence and overall health as her less-than-keen sight and muffled hearing does.

My answer is to make sure that she is with kindly dogs who she can recognise as friends. I also treat her even more gently and considerately than I did before and include a lot of reassuring pats and cuddles, especially at bedtime when I spend fifteen minutes massaging her legs and shoulders and talking soothingly.

Fadey is lucky that I am old, too, and therefore empathetic and understanding of her aches and pains. If she lived with people who only noticed that a nice dog had become an irritable one, without ever thinking about the reasons for the change in behaviour, her life could be a miserable affair.

There is always a reason for a dog changing its pattern of behaviour – it is not because they have become suddenly nasty.

Too often, owners are quite happy to play God when they decide that a bitch needs spaying or a dog castrating. If a dog is aggressive, for example, owners may think well, that's easy, let's just remove the source of the testosterone, but they are, largely, barking up the wrong tree – they should instead be looking for the underlying reasons for the dog's aggression. And, too easily, owners 'put down' their dogs saying, 'It is for their own good.' Yet they exercise very little thought about making their dogs suffer all sorts of other trials and tribulations.

Bob is fifteen and used to be the alpha dog: he had more skill than all of the others and I would guess a lot more brainpower. As I said earlier, he has had the canine equivalent of a stroke and as a result walks rather unsteadily. In addition to this he neither sees nor hears as well as he used to.

He still retains the brainpower to cope with the kennels' busy doggy comings and goings and simply steps back to let his more energetic family members 'do their thing' before continuing on his way. I still guide him through corridors to make sure that he can find his way in the calmest possible fashion.

As you know, at night I put Gemma in with him and make sure that they are both soothed and comfortable before I leave them. Sometimes giving each special treatment can take ages but it's worth it to know I have done all I can.

I used to have four cocker spaniels. One of them, Sally (or to use her full name, Sally Slapcabbage), was a lemon and white whereas her mother was a tricolour and her aunty a blue roan. As a puppy Sally was a bundle of dynamic fun, always dashing here and there with much energy.

My eldest daughter Helen named her and later added the

Slapcabbage because Sally's favourite game was to get the outside leaf of a cabbage from the compost heap and chase around the house and garden shaking it vigorously from side to side. Her siblings would be in hot pursuit of her great prize but Sally always managed to hang on to it until the rest gave up and lay down exhausted. She would then, in what appeared to be an act of triumph, shake the leaf so energetically that it would make loud slapping noises on the wall or the door.

Sally went blind when she was about five years old. I don't remember if it happened gradually or rapidly but in the end she could not see a thing. We kept every single piece of furniture in exactly the same place so that she could apply memory to the layout of every room and she managed to navigate her way around very successfully.

I did not spot any signs of anxiety in her behaviour but that, I believe, was due to the care taken of her by her aunty Tina and her mother Penny – had Sally been an only dog it could well have been different. When we went out in the fields we, at first, put her on an extending lead but soon noticed that the two older dogs kept a close eye on her. We took her off her lead planning to guide her ourselves but were surprised to see, instead, both aunty and mum shepherding her safely across the fields.

The two of them would put their bodies between Sally and a flooded ditch so that she could feel them and then, with nudges, would actively guide her along a safe path. Strangely, indoors they would leave her to her own devices.

Sally never looked anxious, she seemed to accept the fact that she could not see. She, apparently, accepted her lot quite happily with a contentment that belied her condition. Her other senses remained acute and seemed to compensate in part for her loss of sight but it was the care of her doggy companions that made all the difference.

Anxiety is much more about the conditions surrounding the dog than the disadvantage suffered. Dogs cope well with physical limitations but not so well with psychological problems.

Sally died peacefully at just over ten years old, as if she simply went to sleep. I was grateful for this, figuring that she had suffered quite enough during her life without having to suffer a hard death as well. Sometimes there does appear to be some kind of natural justice.

She had remained, for all of her life, one of the jolliest dogs I have ever known. Her passing left a huge hole in my life: for years after her death I found myself still holding doors open for her and calling her, only to be reminded painfully, every time, that she was not there anymore.

When you have a dog your life changes, you find you think about them rather than just thinking of yourself. My lifetime with dogs has been wonderful. They have given back much more than I have given them. I have gone through rare dogless periods and I can't help noting that life without was never as good as life with dogs.

I think that I have been a good trainer and friend because I am prepared to go to any lengths and put the necessary time into understanding what dogs need and how they think.

In the case of Muppet, one of our older Border collies, old age has not yet affected his hearing or sight, but it has turned him into a loner – he simply removes himself and sits and watches the world go by. Now, I watch him closely because his attitude is so different to the busy, precise and always willing sheepdog he once was. He is not showing a great degree of anxiety just yet but the seeds of old age have probably started to grow. I groom him every day, really taking my time and being as soft and reassuring as I possibly can, and I make sure he knows that he has a routine he can live with easily.

As my dogs grow old I change their routine and make it clear to them that rapid response and duty are no longer their concerns – that they can do as they like and I will indulge them.

I notice that the same wit that made them such good working dogs enables them to recognise quickly that whistles and commands are now for the younger and more agile dogs. When the paw of old age beckons, there is no command for 'you don't have to work anymore' but the dogs are quite able to understand my message via, perhaps, my less demanding attitude toward them.

Chapter Ten

How to Settle
a Rescue Dog

First of all, take that vital leap of the imagination and try to see things the way the dog sees them: to be really successful you need to put yourself in its place.

The newly rehomed dog may well have experienced bad treatment and this will have made it vulnerable and, therefore, unpredictable. I take a step backward whenever I am tempted to be over-affectionate toward a strange dog: I know very little about the dog and it knows even less about me and my ways. If its previous owner had no idea how to treat it then the dog will expect no better from me.

*Before you start any sort of training, there
is a greater need – to try as hard as you can
to make your new dog feel relaxed and
as at home as it can be.*

There are very many types of dogs and even more types of families and houses but, whatever your situation, the fundamental principles remain the same.

If your dog is from a rescue centre there will be some information, albeit scant. You will know how it has been fed – the time or times of feeds and the type and quantity of the food for each feed. You can also expect to have a fair idea of the type and times of exercise it has been given.

As you will have seen the dog before you decided to give it a home, you will know what sort of conditions it had been housed in and you might have some idea of how happy or disturbed it was during its stay at the rescue centre.

Don't be afraid to really quiz the people at the rescue centre about your dog's likes and dislikes. The staff will not mind, they want the best for both you and the dog – it is the people who don't ask any questions who worry them; as those who are reluctant to answer your questions should worry you. And a really important tip is to ask all you need to know about the dog before you give staff at a rescue centre any indication that you may like to take it.

Another tip is to take a few minutes to write down what they tell you and keep the details on your computer or in your diary. It is very easy to forget what's been said or, worse, invent information to replace the things you can't remember.

Make a point of gathering as much useful information as possible.

Don't take it for granted that your rescue dog's behaviour will be consistent.

A lady I know resettled a lurcher and really believed that she was making great progress. One day, her cat came in through the window and jumped first on her then stepped on to the lurcher sitting beside her. The dog showed no reaction at all and its owner congratulated herself on the rapid improvement they had made together. The next day, however, the dog very nearly put paid to the cat.

The Reverend Charles Kingsley's book *The Water Babies* describes the less than enlightened Victorian custom of sending little boys up chimneys to clean them. No one asked the little boys if they minded doing it. In Kingsley's fairytale there is a character called Mrs Doasyouwouldbedoneby who, as her name suggests, believes that we should treat others as we would like to be treated. She cuddles the little boys, reads them stories and brings love and comfort in place of the hard lives they have known previously.

I extend Mrs Doasyouwouldbedoneby's philosophy to the way you should treat your dog – too many owners do not have such an enlightened attitude.

Think seriously about the welfare of your dog and realise that the treatment a dog receives is reflected in its behaviour.

Routine Soothes Anxiety

I am a great believer in the all-important discipline of providing a routine for all of my dogs. A dog with a routine is a happy dog because it knows what is going to happen next. A framework that the dog can understand lessens the anxiety it might feel. If it can see what happens next and rely on it the settling-in period will be reduced considerably.

Dogs make their own rituals, which is to say that they perform actions in a set, ordered and repeated fashion. Greeting each other and us in exactly the same way is but one example.

Routine will speed recovery from any trauma or disturbance the rescue dog may have suffered.

Having seen the extent to which their routines benefit my own dogs, I would go so far as to say that routine is almost the Holy Grail in making a dog feel totally at home.

The routine needs to have a good mix of ingredients encompassing food, exercise, cuddles and treats, and sleeping arrangements: regularity and consistency are key.

Food

With a newly rehomed dog keep the routine established by the rescue centre with regard to feeding times and the type and amounts of food. Try to feed the dog in the same place every time – I go as far as using the same words every time as I pass the dish of food to the dog.

For us, with fourteen dogs to feed routine not only makes

the whole process more ordered but also helps the dogs to relax in the knowledge that the pattern does not vary. The last dog to be fed does not pace up and down anxiously wondering whether we have forgotten it because the ritual is so well established it can recognise every step in the procedure.

If after a while you think that some other type of food would be more beneficial for your dog make the change gradually – introduce the new food in small additions as you slowly reduce the old. The same technique of gradual change would apply to all aspects of the dog's life.

You can of course change the feeding routine established by the rescue centre but make sure you do so very slowly indeed.

Bear in mind that some vets sell very expensive specialist foods and this may influence any guidance they might recommend with regard to feeding. For this reason I, personally, would not ask a vet for advice on feeding – one of my favourite sayings is 'butchers seldom recommend fish'.

Exercise
It is sensible to ask staff at the rescue centre whether your new dog is friendly toward other dogs.

Keep to the same times, type and amounts of exercise that the rescue centre employed, at least for the first few weeks. Listen and take note of whatever the centre tells you about how the dog behaves: Does it pull on the lead? Can it be safely let off the lead? Does it come back when called? Most importantly, make sure you know what word or signal did they use to get the dog to come back, stay, lie down and so on. There is nothing but confusion if you use totally different signals. If the dog runs away, fails to respond to your signal to come back and you become more and more irritated, damage will be done to your relationship right from the start.

Once again, do keep to the established routine. I remember being called back to a farm because the dog I had trained for the farmer was taking no notice of his signals. When I asked him to show me how he was calling the dog back he shouted, 'whup' at the top of his voice and the dog ignored him completely.

I asked him to go to the other side of the hedge and shouted the same word to him. The farmer looked puzzled, raised his arms as if to say, 'what on earth do you mean?' and then confirmed his uncertainty saying that he didn't know what I meant.

'Neither does your dog!' I told him. 'He's been taught to respond to "here".'

I always provided new owners with a tape recording of all of my verbal and whistled commands so that they would be in no doubt about what signals the dogs I had trained would respond to. The farmer confessed that he had always shouted 'whup' to every dog he'd had. Worse still, I later discovered that the same word covered all sorts of actions.

When we lived in Devon and I'd criticise some old farmer for not using his indicators before turning off up a track the locals' response would always be that, 'He knows where he lives.' Charmingly olde worlde but really infuriating if you are driving behind them. In a similar vein, imagine how puzzling it must be for the poor dog who receives nonsense signals and is then blamed for not acting on them.

It always amazes me that even normally thoughtful people, who do not understand anything their dog communicates to them, expect their dog to understand every word and sound they make to it. They simply are not trying to imagine the situation from the dog's viewpoint.

We are all in danger of thinking we know all there is to know about the dog. After all, lots of people have them so how hard can it be?

I noticed this morning that our house martins are back – flying around the front porch and between the rafters in the kennels. These little birds have just flown all the way back from sub-Saharan Africa and found precisely the same spot that they occupied so successfully the year before. We know very little about how the house martin manages to do this just as we know very little about the dog and its reasons for doing certain things. The evolutionary process that gave this tiny bird such huge powers and endurance has shaped the dog as well and we have yet to understand it.

Cuddles

Before I give advice I would ask you to look at the way dogs behave toward each other. They certainly do not spend hours cuddling! No, dogs don't cuddle, they give a quick sniff to check that all is well and then they move on. I suspect that the sniff is just confirmation of something they already know. They do, though, lie next to each other with either their legs or their bodies just touching, but this happens only when *they* want to do it.

It is a human tendency to want to cuddle dogs – often far

too much – and probably does more good to the giver than the cuddled.

For a dog that is new to you, too many cuddles too soon are oppressive and even threatening.

And I strongly recommend that you do not let any children in your household smother the newly rehomed dog with cuddles.

Before you accuse me of being some sort of uncaring monster let me emphasise that I cuddle every one of my dogs every hour of every day but the difference is that they have lived with me for a very long time and know me inside out. And I allow them *to come to me* for a fondling because, this way, I know that they actually want that contact with me.

The object of the exercise is to help the dog feel at home as quickly as possible and taking it straight from a rescue centre and then cuddling it to bits will slow down and damage a relationship that has not even started to form, let alone blossom.

If you remain unconvinced, consider how many cuddles your rescue dog probably received when it was an attractive little puppy, then ask yourself whether these have been a lasting feature of its life.

I would recommend enthusiastically that, rather than cuddle your dog, you should groom it.

So enthusiastically, in fact, that I have devoted chapter thirteen to the subject and there I describe exactly how to approach this mutually important, enjoyable and beneficial exercise.

Leaning over a dog that is sitting or lying in its bed (especially if done quickly) is likely to be misunderstood by a nervous dog – seen, even, as the precursor to an attack. A nervous dog will highly likely be frightened rather than comforted.

Go slowly in the cuddles department, and you and your dog will make better and more valuable progress.

Treats

Again, let's look first at how dogs behave toward each other. So, they do not cuddle and neither do they give each other treats all the time.

Dogs eat their food themselves and most certainly would regard giving some to another dog as a totally foreign act. In fact, by giving your dog treats you might be signalling that you are lower than it is in the pecking order. In the dog world only the weak allow other dogs to pinch their food.

Another point I feel I must make is that there is little sense in establishing a feeding routine if you then blur the edges by continually giving your dog treats and titbits outside normal feeding times.

Dogs were not designed to be browsers nibbling at food all the time and in the wild they glut themselves when food is available. They have evolved as carnivores and thus their digestive system functions best when they are fed as such.

Do not feed your dog tasty morsels from your plate during meal times. This leads to the dog developing a most antisocial food-scrounging habit that it will become compulsive about.

I must admit to being absolutely not in favour of treats. Treats are bribes and eventually become no more than tacit confirmation that this is the only way you can control your dog. The only thing that treats tell a dog is that there is more where the last one came from and that there is no need to do anything you ask of it until after the customary treat has been given.

When it comes to treats, the key word is **scarce***.*

As soon as they become an everyday happening treats stop being appreciated, so the very word is a nonsense. If a dog is off colour, ill or appears depressed then treats are another matter entirely.

Selecting the right sleeping place
I would take great care over choosing a sleeping place for the newly arrived dog. Bear in mind that it has been sleeping in an indoor run or kennel all the time it has been living at a rescue centre. Find out how long it has been at the rescue centre and you will have some idea of how accustomed it is

to that particular situation, then try to make your dog's new sleeping place as similar to that as possible.

There are a lot of fashionable buzzwords in the dog-training world, one is 'holistic' which only too often is said but rarely thought about. It means all of everything, so with a dog it is physical, mental and social.

Houses are very noisy places. We get used to them because it is how we live.

If you stop and think how many noise-producing machines we surround ourselves with you will be surprised. If you count those capable of making high-frequency sounds painful to a dog you will find there are more than you thought there were.

Before you start thinking that dog ownership demands that you purge yourself of all labour-saving and entertainment machines let me reassure you that of course you don't need to. It would be wise though (holistic even) when picking a nice place for your dog to sleep that you 'punch' them all into the equation.

I would always try to pick a quiet corner away from passing feet so that your dog can find a peaceful hiding place away from all the household's hurly burly.

Give your dog a sleeping place that is as far away as possible from the blare of a radio, the jangle of telephones ringing and the noise of vacuum cleaners, dishwashers and washing machines.

And remember, too, that dogs can also be unsettled by worrying demonstrations of changing human moods.

My observations tell me that a lot of my dogs prefer their outside kennels where they can be quiet and private but to try to use an outdoor kennel in an urban area would probably not be advisable as it can be noisier outside than in.

If you do live in quiet countryside and have tried your new dog on an inside bed in every available location, but with no success, then consider seriously an outside kennel and run. The kennel needs to be well insulated and heated. As I mentioned earlier, mine have infrared lambing lights set by time switch to come on for fifteen minutes every hour during cold weather. In all there are three blocks of kennels and each block adjoins its own large, gravel yard. There is also a hay store where bales are stacked to leave corridors and attractive corners for any dog that decides to vary their sleeping habits.

I emphasise strongly that the kennel needs to serve as a bedroom, not a round-the-clock prison.

My dogs have constant company from their pack so they are not going to be lonely and become depressed. No dog should ever be banished to round-the-clock solitary confinement. A dog left outside on its own for long periods of time can quickly develop more behavioural problems than it started with.

If your new dog has a field day when you go out and chews, knocks down flower pots and steals the Sunday joint plus all the other mischief an imprisoned dog can get up to, or if your dog is simply unhappy when left on its own, then an outdoor kennel and run can be good for both of you.

Common sense and dog training are not synonymous, even though they should be, but to avoid all of these problems by using outside quarters seems like a pretty sensible and direct piece of logic to me.

Settling a Rescue Dog: the Basics

- Remember, a rescue dog can be vulnerable and inconsistent.
- Try to understand the dog by putting yourself in its place.
- Gather as much information about the dog as possible.
- Keep to a routine for all things.
- Same food at same time(s).
- Same exercise at same time(s).
- Go easy on the cuddles until the dog really knows you.
- Do not get into the 'treats' habit.
- Choose a sleeping place your dog is happy with.

Chapter Eleven

The Language of the Dog

When I first started working with Border collies my interest was concerned with how well they could understand my commands in order that, together, we could bring back sheep effectively and complete a precise, complex arena demonstration before a large audience. In other words, it was task orientated.

As I progressed my area of interest extended to trying to understand what the dogs were saying to me. Without that, we had only one-way communication and we would thus reach, at best, only half of our full potential.

It stands to reason that a dog that is dominated will do half-heartedly what is asked of it, but if you can make the dog a willing partner then a much greater performance is possible. My dogs were good at what they did because they actually enjoyed doing it.

Because I worked up to nine dogs simultaneously I used a different language or dialect Welsh, German, a Devon burr, and so on – to give each dog its commands so that each dog would know when I was talking to it.

The method of training was to teach each dog on its own, away from the others, so that it would recognise the sound of the commands in the language specific to it.

Added to this fairly complicated procedure were two other methods of communication, body language and whistles. The body language not only varied with each dog but also with the conditions we might be working in.

There is good reason for my use of three methods of communication: body language enabled me to work the dogs on the cliff tops of North Devon during a blasting wind when they would have heard neither whistle nor voice; the whistle, on a still day, could be heard a couple of miles away so it was good for distance work on a still day; and the voice I used when the dogs were working close to me.

If you feel like congratulating me for performing like a busker playing several instruments at the same time you would be wasting your praise, spare a thought for my dogs: they had to learn body-language signs, then the spoken language equivalent, then the whistle equivalent of both.

I connected the three forms by slowly building up in

layers so that the commands were clearly linked. At the beginning of training the dog would learn the body movement, this was followed some weeks later by the spoken word and, much later, that would be followed by the whistle. It did not take too long for the dogs to realise that each version of a given command meant the same thing.

Body Language

So, layer by layer: body language; body language and word; body language, word and whistle. Thinking about it, I had actually stumbled upon the same system a wild dog would use so it was a natural way for my dogs to learn. Wild dogs use three types of signal: when they are at their base or home they use body language and quiet noises, further away voice and at far distances a high-pitched howl, much like my whistle.

My first lead dog, Bob, learned to understand all the other dogs' languages in both whistle and word but only took notice of the body language reserved for him. I think he realised that my unconscious body language could be relied on as a true reflection of what was really happening and, as it referred to him and me and no other, it was, in real terms, the only version worth noting.

Does your dog understand every word you say? I also pose this very question in *The Dog Whisperer* and the answer, of course, is a resounding No. But your dog will understand almost every body-language signal you consciously or unconsciously make.

Body language is the main means of communication for the dog.

I must stress that when giving working demonstrations each dog was expected to move with absolute precision, no more and no less than was signalled. One main observation emerges from this – the dog is a much more sophisticated creature than those who do not work them might realise. It is only in the exacting area of working with a dog that you appreciate the full extent of its capabilities, and though to work a dog is probably not your aim the lessons learned are certainly relevant.

I have noted before that dogs are much more able to understand what we are saying to them than we are at understanding whatever they may try to convey to us. Whether or not the obstacle to this communication is our pride in the supposed superiority of the human race I can't say, but I suspect that it has much to do with it.

Of course dogs listen to our voices but it is their highly developed ability to read what we really mean by the position of our bodies that makes their understanding so acute.

I remember my friend Jonathan Marshall, an accomplished and enormously entertaining falconer, telling a hawk to sit on a telegraph pole next to the one it was already sitting on. I watched Jon carefully to see if he gave some small body language clue to the hawk.

He repeated the trick several times during the display, every time with his back to the bird. As the hawk could not understand his language it must have been responding to some change in his body position but it was beyond my most attentive scrutiny. Animals and birds have an

136

amazing ability to read our intention even before we speak it.

I have read several books on how dogs speak and have found that I do not agree with any of them. I believe their 'translations' and interpretations are far too simplistic and that the dog's language is more complex than most experts suggest.

Getting the Right End of the Stick

Let me start by explaining the nature of dog communication. Dogs speak to us, and each other, mainly by expression, posture and movement.

Consider the human posture compared to how dogs stand. Under normal circumstances and in good health, we have two legs and we stand upright, head erect, shoulders relaxed, back straight. We know what that 'normal' posture is and can thus make judgements about a person's mood, intentions and physical health based on their posture and the way in which they move – from aggression to shyness to joy. Facial expression, too, can send clear signals: eyes opened wide usually indicate alert interest; eyes narrowed might indicate irritation, and so on.

The dog is built to stand four square, its head and neck comfortably positioned so that its weight is distributed equally between each leg. If it is not standing like this, its abnormal stance may well indicate physical discomfort.

As the dog moves from its four square position, that movement sends a readily understood message to any other dog in the vicinity: neck comes forward, tail stretched out – it is about to run; neck comes forward, tail in its usual position – it is going to walk forwards. It is a matter of comfortable, natural balance and recognising the physical clues to what's about to happen.

Reading the Face, Tail and Neck

In addition to overall posture, three parts of the dog's anatomy carry most of the messages to other dogs and to humans: the head, particularly the face, the tail and the neck.

The face would at first seem the most obviously expressive – the thing that will give most messages – but the tail more often than not works in partnership with the face, so watching both gives the most information.

Lips drawn back to show the teeth is often a clear sign of aggression that is likely to be followed by action but I have two dogs that 'grin' in a way that looks very much like a snarl to anyone who does not know them. Lips drawn back, teeth showing plus hackles standing up is likely to indicate aggression created by fear so, defence rather than attack is likely. Hackles up, lips drawn back, eyes narrowed, ears lying back against the head and body forming as narrow a target as possible, together with a deliberate, slow walk toward its intended victim does mean the dog is angry and it's in attack mode – if it does all this minus the walk forward this is a warning and, at this point, my best advice would be to back off. Muzzle furrowed enough to look like a snarl but without fully exposing the teeth is a warning to back off. Head up, eyes wide open plus an open mouth indicates interest and if you add a vigorously wagging tail then, you know what is being said. If it rushes toward you with its mouth wide open puffing and panting with its tail wagging so hard that it also moves its body off balance then friend dog is a friend indeed.

Head up, eyes wide open, mouth closed means attention but also uncertainty.

If any dog's tail is tucked under its belly it either does not feel well or has been frightened. I think bitches suffer from pre-menstrual tension and a tail tucked under the belly can also indicate that a female is coming into season.

My point in telling you this is so that you realise you already know most of this body language and most messages that your dog sends you will be through its physical appearance and movement rather than the noises it makes.

Barking

Of course there is barking as well: the repeated, high-pitched bark that asks you to throw the ball again or the deeper bark, punctuated by pauses, that tells you a stranger is near – and, correctly interpreted, can even tell you how close they are and how well the dog totally or partly knows who it is.

A string of deep-toned barks hardly punctuated by gaps says that the intruder, or the disturbance, is close. A series of still deeper barks with long pauses between them means your dog has heard someone or something and needs to put in those quiet pauses so that it can pinpoint proximity and direction plus work out who or what is coming.

A mile or so away from where we live is a hotel that holds wedding receptions during which fireworks are set off.

When the fireworks go off it is obvious from the dogs' barking pattern that fear of the noise is their main concern – there are no pauses between barks and it's as if the dogs understand that the noise will not come any nearer. The barking pattern is different when they sense a person on the move.

Misty, you may remember is a wonderful lesson in using brain over brawn when working sheep. She is, however, awful at playing a part in a demonstration because she seems to think it her role to break the other dogs' concentration – she virtually dances in front of them. She makes it quite clear that she regards the whole thing as a game that needs to be played by her rules rather than mine.

If she stands too close to my lead demonstration dog, Susie, then Susie refuses to move because Misty's closeness would reduce her options. Misty then calls out with a series of puppy-type, high-pitched yelps designed to communicate with both Susie and me. To Susie she is saying, 'Come on, MOVE,' to me the communication is also eminently clear, 'Come on, *make* her move.' Misty's excitement at chasing Susie far outweighs the satisfaction she might gain from demonstrating her skills.

Learning to Be a Dog

Watch a mother dog with her litter of puppies and the main communication currency is obvious – body language. When the puppies are very small the mother makes very few sounds – all of the communication with the puppies is by body shape. She will use her body shape to encourage them to the milk bar or to gather them within her warmth and protection but little else. Of course in the early stages puppies can't see, so her 'language' is simple and straight-forward.

As the puppies grow and move toward eating solids the sound part of mother's communication with them will increase, but not by very much. When they are ready to be weaned the mother will regurgitate food for them, the sound of her retching and the pungent smell that follows signal food to the pups. By now, the puppies have teeth and much better coordination, and will have fully opened and focused their eyes – they can clearly see her facial expressions and they are more boisterous and investigative.

This is the first, real, intensive learning period of a dog's life. This is when they learn about what it is to be a dog from the ideal teacher – another dog – and this is the most important time in the puppy's development.

A puppy taken away from its mother too early might well miss out on important parts of her teaching and that could reflect badly on the dog's behaviour in the future.

If a dog has never learned to live in a dog family what chance does it stand of adapting to yours? The mother not only feeds her puppies' bodies, she also feeds their minds with a lot of information. If they bite too hard on her teat she scowls quite dreadfully as well as making a rumbling noise and her meaning is clear. If one of her litter wanders too far away her head comes up and she fixes it with a fierce stare, reinforced with a growl.

While the puppies are learning to be dogs, mother communicates almost exclusively using body language and making, on the whole, threatening, 'stop that at once' kind of statements. She will loom over the puppies, or stiffen her body, or stare them straight in the eye and growl.

Dogs remember these lessons throughout adulthood so – providing the dog recognises you as senior to it – a growl, a grimace and a stiff-legged movement toward it will communicate your displeasure much more clearly than a string of words that it does not understand.

That the mother relies on body language is understand-able when you look back to the dog's wild ancestry – silence would keep her litter safer from predators. And dogs hunting prey are not going to waste their energy and breath making noises when there are more efficient ways to communicate. Even the wolf stops running in order to howl out location signals.

If your dog is close to you use body language as a silent command if it is further away use voice and if it is a long way away use a high-pitched sound either by whistle or by voice. These three methods are in the true context of a dog's use of its own language.

In my kennels the adult dogs use mainly body language to

communicate with one another. There is, now and again, an outbreak of high-pitched barking so explicit that, wherever I am in the house, not only do I know who is barking but also who they are barking at and why – it is as clear a communication to me as it is to the dogs.

Dogs do not hold prolonged dog-to-dog 'conversations'; people, however, do. As I said in chapter four, people need to talk in order to exchange information gathered from a selection of sources, from newspapers and television to e-mails and mobile phones. A dog's world, you'll recall, is different. Dogs are concerned with the here and now and because their senses – such as smell and hearing – are so well developed they all know what's going on around them at the same time and therefore have no need to vocalise that information.

When the pack is together at home, their main interest is their inter-relationships because that affects the pack's wellbeing. A series of agitated yipping noises coming from the kennels would indicate that Polly and Susie are having some sort of spat and will be running back and forth along the fence that separates them. There is a locked gate between the dogs and I know this particular yipping means this is a mock, ritualistic confrontation.

Actions Speak Louder than Words

Actions are another means by which dogs communicate. For example, a young dog not yet house trained might well respond to an over-fierce owner by wetting the floor. This is usually puppy behaviour.

Let me illustrate how communication can go awry when it comes to house training. Imagine your new dog has been with you long enough to know what sort of people it is living with and knows that one of you is quiet and gentle and quite prepared to allow the dog time to learn that wetting the floor is not done, while the other is impatient and insistent that the dog learns immediately.

The impatient person rubs the dog's nose in the mess it has made, mistakenly believing that this treatment will produce a rapid improvement. The dog's reaction to this will be to wet the floor more often, simply because it is frightened of the fiercer of the two people and is telling them so by demonstration. Translated into human speech, the puppy is telling them something like, 'Please be gentle, I am only a puppy.' (Puppies wet the floor and their mother cleans it up.)

So, the correct reaction to your puppy wetting the floor should be to understand why and thus realise, perhaps for the first time, that your dog is frightened of you. How do you know this? Because your dog clearly told you so!

Patience is certainly a virtue in this situation and a gentle approach will bring much quicker results – taking a fierce approach will only make the problem much worse and cause it to become ingrained.

A Smattering of Dog Language and How to Interpret It

Jumping up
Though not desirable if it's big and strong or muddy the dog is being friendly. Bearing in mind how tall we are compared

to them the only way they can get close to our faces is by jumping up – important to our dogs as they glean much about our reaction to them from our facial expressions. This is where breath indicates the state of our health and much information about our wellbeing can be learned.

The dog's desire to jump up could hark back to when it was a hungry, newly weaned puppy jumping up to nudge its mother's mouth in the hope she'd regurgitate and feed it. This regurgitation memory is also why dogs eat food that another has vomited. It might seem pretty disgusting to us but it is a natural survival instinct in a dog.

Jumping up is not in essence an aggressive act as there are much more sensible areas for a dog to bite without it exposing its whole body to a possible attack. Never say 'never', though, because in a different context the jumping-up could escalate into something more dangerous with potentially serious consequences. I would not in any circumstances encourage a dog to jump up at a child; the dog may consider the child to be a puppy and one rough game encouraged can easily lead to another much rougher one.

Paw poking

Some experts say a dog that paws your leg is trying to dominate. This is absolute nonsense. If it wanted to, the dog would dominate by rather fiercer methods than a bit of paw poking. When your dog is poking your leg with a paw it's a reminder that your dog wants more attention.

I have two dogs who would be regarded as low in the pack pecking order and both specialise in the paw poking, 'pay attention to me' communication – which I find most endearing unless, of course, I am wearing smarter clothes than usual. Both these paw-pokers (mother and son) show their teeth in what I call a 'grin'. Some might mistake this expression for aggression but it is, in fact, saying, 'I'm not too sure of myself' and a plea for reassurance. It is often accompanied by the dog bending its body as though it would like to wrap itself around my legs.

Any dog planning an act of aggression will set up his body position to ensure the best chance of success – it will not waste time and effort bending. Intention of an aggressive nature is preceded by absolute stillness and by staring, unblinking, at the target. I have already described (Reading the Face, Tail and Neck) in detail the language of the dog demonstrating aggression, warning or about to attack.

Eye contact

My largest dog, Barney, is almost as big as a Newfoundland but for all his size and strength he lacks the confidence of some of my smaller dogs. He is particularly worried by direct eye contact, especially when we are uncomfortably close to each other and, most particularly, when I am kneeling and our heads are at the same height.

A kiss on the face would turn him into a quivering jelly or perhaps a more dangerously defensive dog. He regards my mouth with the greatest suspicion and is not at all sure about my motives.

We enter into the outer margins of his fear area when I am grooming him. Barney has a very long coat which tends to get tangled and full of snags, twigs and whatever other extraneous bits and pieces he has picked up running through undergrowth so grooming happens often.

We go through the same routine every time. He looks me in the eye to see if I am looking into his. If I am, he will hold my gaze for just seconds then he quickly chooses the easy way out and rolls on to his back – which is submission.

This, in fact, is an example of the dog's ability to be rather more subtle than most dog trainers would suggest. Here, Barney is only using the submission posture as a device to see if it can alter what looks to him like threatening language from me.

At moments when Barney is feeling most alarmed he will show his teeth. This has nothing to do with aggression, it is about nervousness.

His wide-eyed, unblinking stare that seems as though he is looking into my very soul is, also, not a sign of aggression. It does not mean that he is on maximum alert, rather he is examining me closely in order to see what I might do next.

Barney and I have a strange relationship unlike any that I have with my other dogs. He regards me as a big dog capable of giving him a hard time and he's going to be watching me for the rest of his life to make sure that I do not overstep his margins of acceptability. In other words, he would rather rely on his judgement of me and his prediction of my next action than be distracted or charmed by my soothing words. He is not prepared to be lulled into a sense of false security by my verbal attempts to put him at ease.

*I am gently allaying his fears by lowering
my head so that he can sniff my hair and
be reassured that all is safe because it is
still the same old Dad.*

At night when I put him to bed I walk into his kennel with him and stroke him and talk soothingly so that he will learn that even in a confined space he is totally safe with me. Barney has been like this for years so I do not expect him to change but I can at least make these close-quarter encounters more comfortable for him.

Where his fear came from I do not know but I do understand what he is saying to me, which is something like, 'I like you but I am not totally sure of you.'

Every single thing a dog does carries a reason and the reason is most often a desire to communicate with other dogs or with people.

Aiming high

I have heard the tree described as an information centre for dogs where all the latest news is posted.

Male dogs cock their legs up trees in order to advertise themselves, and the higher they aim, the better because that tells other male dogs that this is one big dog it's best not to tangle with, and tells every female in the area that here is an attractive, likely suitor.

A friendship game

I have noticed that dogs in my pack have what I would describe in human terms, special friends. Between the dogs who become particularly close to one another, a skittish game of shunting is played. One dog will put both its front feet together and skitter forward, in a jerky way, toward the friend. This is an obvious plea for a game that can, when the time is ripe, be a mating ritual or a kind of foreplay but at all other times is the equivalent of a declaration of friendship.

In the kitchen, Misty will behave in the same way to me, especially if I am suggesting something pleasant such as a walk, and at the same time she also gives exaggerated puffs. Put it all together and she's saying something like, 'Let's do it, I really fancy it!'

There are, of course, many more examples of the dog's language but the few I have described will, I hope, make you more aware that an awful lot of (mostly silent) communication – 'talking', if you will, is going on.

How Does Your Dog Read You?

You, too, are talking to your dog – communicating with it all the time through your body language and the things you do. Fast actions mean danger; slam a door or bang down a saucepan and the dog knows you are in a bad mood; walk stiffly and it reads aggression or irritation; a relaxed gait says 'good mood'.

*Your dog reads every move you make
and every move spells out to it your
mood and intent.*

In our training field there are ferns that intend to exile the grass and take over the world so, every day I take a swishy stick and knock off the tops to give other plants a chance of flourishing. My dogs know why I have the stick and are unconcerned by the fern bashing but if I bang a fence rail with it they take that as a warning I might be dangerous. If I'm carrying a crook they know that means we are about to work.

The more you understand about dogs and the way they communicate the quicker you will progress with settling in your dog and training it. And with growing awareness and understanding of everything your dog is telling you comes an ever deeper and more mutually rewarding relationship with your dog.

All my dogs understand me and I always understand them – and each other. This mutual confidence in communication, obviously, makes for a very comfortable relationship. We can concentrate on the pure pleasure of a walk, for example, and when I ask the dogs to do something, I use their language.

In the middle of writing, I popped down to our kennels. Sally was lying on a big pile of hay under the lean-to. Because she knew that I was just passing through she 'grinned' at me by showing her teeth but remained lying down and did no more than move her front feet as though preparing to stand up. The communication was not only clear, 'I'm pleased to see you', but impressive because, by not getting up, she showed she knew I wouldn't be staying.

There is a great awareness with dogs. When Maureen was heavily pregnant with Helen, our yellow Labrador, Sugar Ray, who had always pulled when on a lead, appeared to sense my wife's vulnerability. When walking with me he continued to 'pull for England' but the minute Maureen took his lead he would walk, entirely of his own accord, gently by her side.

As a, separate, point of interest, Sugar Ray always refused, point blank, to take the short cut home through the cemetery. Even if it was pouring with rain and the cemetery path would have saved me a full five minutes, he insisted that we walk around it. I will not try to explain his behaviour except to say that there is much more to the dog than meets the eye.

Non-verbal Commands

If you can't get your dog to stop and stand with a verbal command try, instead, walking forward and coming to a decisive stop, dragging your foot along the ground for emphasis. If you want the dog to behave, try walking forward stiffly toward it.

If you want to reassure, hold out your arms as if to embrace.

If you want the dog to move to the left, or right, try turning your head and your gaze sharply in the direction you want it to go. It probably won't happen first time but the dog will quickly come to fully understand what you are silently communicating.

When Maureen and I were learning German we made a point of speaking only German for an hour each day and it improved our ability no end.

Try setting aside a period of time each day when the language you and your dog communicate in is purely non-verbal.

Being mute might hamper you at first but very quickly you'll discover that you are communicating with your dog and perhaps even more eloquently than you have been with words.

You may have seen performances in which a woman dances with her dog? This shows just how responsive dogs are to body movement. The human dance partner supplies both rhythm and choreography and the dog reads the messages the handler is sending, not by voice or by music, but by her body movement.

The process required to achieve this level of understanding is neither easy nor quick but relies on repeating the various moves, over and over again, then fitting the dance to the music.

Chapter Twelve

Ceri's Progress

If ever you needed proof of what I am saying here it is.

I had, by now, been training Ceri every day for four weeks. We trained using short, ten-minute sessions and concentrated on achieving a quicker response to the body language I was using to direct him.

I'd reasoned that, while I would follow the one-brick-at-a-time rule with a dog who was not nervous, any fine focus and insistence that he should master a single action – such as stand, sit, and so on – before moving on to the next would be rather too demanding for my friend Ceri. His nervous nature precludes such an approach.

With Ceri, lingering too long on one command would look dangerously like serious intent rather than a game, and this would be counterproductive to training. Ceri knows me well and trusts – albeit with that watchful eye – that my intentions and treatment toward him are good. Nevertheless, his response to a game will always be better because he sees it as non-threatening.

There is no formula that covers every single dog, especially when it comes to a potentially fragile rescue dog that may have been damaged by a previous unsatisfactory relationship.

You may well find you that you need, first, to establish a trusting relationship with your dog before beginning training that will help both of you to enjoy life together.

If your dog really dislikes training then take more time to build a good, trusting relationship before you start the work of training.

Recap: the Key Points of Training a Nervous Dog

The art of training a nervous dog is that it never recognises the procedure as training but regards it as an enjoyable game.

It is important that instructions are delivered with a light and cheerful voice and that harsh tones, caused by irritation never creep in.

If you do become irritated, stop the training session. A command issued in an irritated way can mean arresting progress as well as throwing away the developing feeling of trust between you and your dog.

Dogs cannot be fooled, and any inconsistency in your attitude, such as a cheerful voice accompanied by irritation in your body language, will be quickly spotted – and it will be the irritation in your body language that is noticed, the cheerful voice ignored.

If your rescue dog had a traumatic experience with its previous owner then patience and taking training slowly will be the only way to move forward. And a consistent approach is vital. In this sense, dogs are a little like children. Ever read a child a story and suddenly decided to change the ending to make it more exciting? Not a good move.

Children like a pattern or routine that varies as little as possible – and so do dogs. So, that means tying the command to precisely the same movements every single time or, with a word command, using the same word with the same tone of voice every time. Repetition makes perfect.

To reiterate, you are communicating to your dog all the time through body language, tone of voice and the things you do, such are the ways our dogs read our intentions.

Signs, Signals and Repetition

Let's say, for example, that you are in the habit of watching the news on television, with the dog in the room, before you go to bed. When the news comes to an end the dog will get up and prepare to go out, not because it recognises the music that signals the programme's end and not because the dog has an in-built clock, but because when *you* recognise the sign off you have a reflex reaction to it – you might give a sigh, or stretch or maybe just shift position in your chair.

Whether you are aware of it or not, you likely react the same way every night and this is what tells the dog that your viewing has finished and it's time for bed.

Certain signs you make, however subtle, however small, become synonymous with specific intentions and your dog is a past master at reading them.

When I return home from a walk with Misty and Ben – the dogs that live in the house with us – I open the door then step back. It is me stepping back that tells them they are expected to go inside, and that they are going first. Having monitored this series of events day after day I've noted that the open door signals to them that it's *possible* to go into the house but it doesn't mean that we *are* going in – they wait until I step back before attempting to enter. This tells me they are watching every move I make and, furthermore, choosing which movements are relevant and warrant an action by them.

It stands to reason then that, through repetition, other signals will also be just as easily understood.

My sheepdogs have always been able to single out the one sheep in a flock of several hundred that is going to cause problems. A predator, such as lion, a cheetah or, indeed, a pack of Africa's rare, wild Cape hunting dogs, will select the weakest animal in a herd – be it old, young or injured – which offers the best chance of a kill. They know.

If dogs were hunting together they would not continually crash into each other because they can read each other's body language. In fact they make small signs to indicate which way they are going.

Have you noticed that very many dog owners crouch down and hold out their arms to encourage their dog to come to them? It seems to be a universal signal, as is patting the leg. For much the same reason, we crouch before young children when they are learning to walk – encouraging them to take one more step. The dog runs between its owner's outstretched arms in order to receive a fuss, the child takes one more step knowing it is safe.

On the whole, dog owners make this gesture without thinking and dogs understand its implication very quickly. The dog owners do not need to tell the dog, 'Come, and I'll make a fuss of you' – body language communicates the message.

These simple gestures and routines I have been talking about warrant more attention than they tend to be given: I study them because communicating with dogs is my business and my passion and so I need to know the best signals.

It is worth noting that during training sessions – or at any other time for that matter – a dog will almost always find an opportunity to do something that will irk you. But a dog that repeatedly and stubbornly does something you really don't want it to do also presents a real opportunity as well as honing your ability as a trainer.

Sometimes, whatever mischief it might get up to tells you far more than a trouble-free progression through a training routine will. And though it might seem like a setback at the time, the information you may gain from the misdemeanour may work to your advantage in the long term. After all the real reason you have a dog is because you love it and the more you learn about it the greater that love will be.

Ceri: the Willing Pupil

When I talk about you walking and stopping I am talking about teaching your dog to read and respond to your silent language. After thirty, ten-minute sessions in which I was walking, stopping, then waiting, Ceri was producing a pretty good performance and mirroring what I was doing quite faithfully. I did start to add the occasional word signal for emphasis, especially when his response was lackadaisical but body language was the essence.

In the early stages of training it is important to let the dog know that you are always watching it.

Dogs are always very conscious of whether or not you are paying them serious attention and will put much more into the training if they can sense your intent.

As I have said before I never use treats in the form of a bribe. Dogs are quite intelligent enough to follow instructions. Treats are a distraction. Some experts say that a dog's intelligence is equivalent to that of a four-year-old child. I can't imagine any school or parent rewarding children with a treat every time they do something good. Perhaps that is why there are so many overweight dogs around?

Using treats to reward every small success is irrelevant in the context of training and is likely to hamper any hopes of training achieving satisfying results.

The Training Programme: What We Achieved in Month One

Each session lasted no longer than ten minutes and embraced just the two aims described below (can be done with the dog on or off a lead):

Aim: To follow my chosen direction by dint of my body language signals.

Method: I concentrated on walking, say, ten yards and then turned dramatically (or in an exaggerated way), retraced my steps and then repeated the movement about four or five times.

What did we achieve?

Ceri did stay close to me and turned when I turned.

Once we got to this stage, I started on the groundwork for the most important tool in the dog trainer's kit – the instruction to 'come back'.

Aim: To recognise the 'come back' signal – again signalled by body language.

Method: Ceri was never far away for this exercise as it will work better when the dog is relatively near and not being led astray by some deliciously tempting sniff. I crouched on my haunches and held out my arms so that he would know to come back and then made a huge fuss of him every time he did.

What did we achieve?

A pretty good result considering that there were no voice commands.

A long and luxurious grooming followed each training session – a much better reward than treats as it also cements bonding.

So, you can see that after thirty sessions of just ten minutes each what seemed at first like very little has grown to become an important foundation for what will follow.

Emphasise the Essentials

During the second month of training I plan to add voice commands to make clear and emphasise essentials such as 'come back' or 'stay'.

Commands that relied on body language alone will be reinforced by verbal signals delivered at the same time so, hand signal plus a spoken 'come here'.

My aim is to supply a layered system of training with a link between body language, the spoken word and the whistle or call. There is a real need for the dog to understand all three so that my dog and I are always totally in touch with one another.

Jack of No Trades

As they would say in the Eurovision Song Contest: Jack? *Nul points*. It is as if there are two separate strands to Jack, one is happy and near to normal, the other is a mixed-up vulnerability. And the two strands crisscross and tangle with each other to the extent that I never know which version of Jack I have before me

The only change I have seen in him so far is that the happy Jack is, for the first time, overpowering his vulnerable side – though by a barely discernible margin. And, to be honest, happy is too strong a word: better to describe him as more at ease.

He has made progress but it is tiny, and most certainly not cemented in place. Usually the lessons learned add a thin skin of confidence and each new achievement makes the skin thicker and more likely to last. Dear old Jack's confidence (if there at all) is ephemeral.

We established at the start that Jack – unlike ninety-nine per cent of his breed – is not motivated by movement or the prospect of a more exciting life made so by work well done.

I have spotted no 'magic buttons' that will turn Jack from tractor into racing car. There have been (as yet) no revelations, no valuable information that will make possible a short cut to greater things. Perhaps trying to achieve a racing car is where my training is going wrong? Jack might be happier to be a tractor. Happiness, after all, is one of the training's original aims.

I am by nature fairly stubborn and do not take kindly to giving up or changing direction. To take the latter course is close to admitting defeat.

> *The evidence in front of my eyes is*
> *that Jack will never make a worker,*
> *he never has been and it looks likely*
> *that he never will be.*

The more I struggle to find a way for him the more I discover that my frustration is not as great as I'd expect it to be and that the love I have for him grows instead of shrinking. Each time we get it wrong I find I like him more and I try harder to find a system that he will be happy with.

Over the first month I tried the directional walking, the turning and stopping, over and over again, only to observe that Jack was observing me – as though this mysterious set of movements was designed to amuse rather than teach.

Sometimes, begrudgingly, he produced a kind of sloppy response, but always half-hearted and without willingness. And to rub it all in he did it all with a hangdog expression rather than keen attentiveness.

He did, however, do enough to tell me that what I am trying to teach him is not beyond him but simply either boring in the extreme, or too frightening – given a little more time I shall sort out which of these two it is.

Objectively and without passion I would say that my training direction is wrong for Jack and as much as I dislike having to admit it, his intelligence is different from any sheepdog I have met (and there have been rather more than just a few). Most certainly, he is no less intelligent than my other dogs but something, yet to be discovered, is acting as a barrier between him and me.

We have made progress, or at least I think we have, in directions that I would not have expected. When all the dogs are out in the training field Jack does something that he never used to do: he watches me intently all the time. He does not have the confidence to come up close to watch me, he keeps his distance – outside the danger area where he might be included in my dastardly plans. But, significantly, Jack *is* watching me.

This body language is telling me something and I think I know, in part, what it might be. On an obvious level there is relief for Jack when he is out with the other dogs because it takes the pressure off him to perform. My attention on him is inevitably less because I have all the others to watch. I also note that he is bright enough to have noticed this!

This tells me that it is the demand, or pressure on him, that is hampering our progress. It is my frighteningly singular attention on him that is putting him off.

But he has learned to watch. I shall think hard about this.

Jack Has Moved On

A couple of other changes have happened, too. When we come back from a particularly rainy walk I always dry each of my dogs. Our Aga spends most of the day covered in drying towels during wet weather.

Jack used to absent himself from the queue of waiting dogs, all of whom push themselves forward in a 'me first' attempt for the ministration of a warm towel – not Jack, he'd sneak back into his kennel. 'Sneak' is a good description for he'd be there one minute and gone the next. The vanishing dog.

Now, he waits in full view for his turn as though he has just begun to consider that he deserves a dry as much as the others do. When I start to dry him he shows signs of really enjoying it whereas before he would do anything to avoid it. He also, now, comes up to be groomed whereas in the past he would have gone out of his way to avoid this.

I am going to follow a hunch and during the next month will put emphasis on different areas of Jack's training. Instead of trying to achieve progress in a formal way I am going to employ some lateral thinking and see if I can come at the problem from a different direction.

There is a lesson here for you as well as for me: don't get impatient if your dog is not becoming the blueprint of what you had in mind.

Don't force it, don't keep insisting but bend with the wind and the reality of the situation and stay both kind and patient. Frustration, or any sign of it, will ruin everything.

Chapter Thirteen

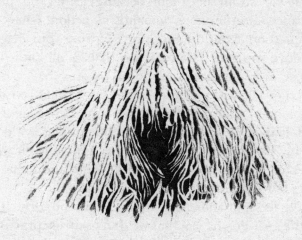

In Praise of Grooming

A doctor once told me that he never told people what he did for a living especially if they were newly met at a party or some other social gathering. According to him, the minute people knew what he did they would ask him about their bad backs or other aches and pains so his social life turned into a busman's holiday.

When friends discover that I was once a vicar and therefore might know a little about theology they ask questions. The word theology derives from the Greek and, in essence, means the study of things divine. They tend to ask obscure questions, usually about the Old Testament or some little-known prophet. Favourite questions are usually concerned with the unanswerable or ones where knowing the answer will put no strain on them because it has no practical significance and therefore demands no action. I have never had a question about the meaning of loving your neighbour as you love yourself. The reason is that we all know what it means or, more accurately, we think we do.

Whether you are religious or not the practical wisdom of this statement from Jesus himself can be recognised as absolutely true. If we loved our neighbours the world would be a truly wonderful place. (You must ask yourself whether you would include dogs in this commandment which appears to be aimed primarily at humankind . . .)

I have thought about this often and am puzzled. If we all know the answer why is it that we don't actively practise it? If we did we would change the world for the better.

The reason we don't practise it is that it is too difficult and, if the truth is known, we can't really be bothered. The line itself is short, as are the words that make it up. There is nothing complicated about it whatsoever but we just can't (or won't) do it. Maybe it is because we are frightened that others would not play by the same rules and would take advantage of us?

I use this example because it reminds me very much of some students of dog psychology and behaviour who just love complicated questions but don't look to answer the simple ones that are right under their noses.

Often, deep and real wisdom can be found in the shortest and simplest of observations.

A lot of dog behaviourists and students of canine psychology reach enthusiastically for each new idea as though it were some kind of panacea. Of course it would be invidious of me to name the inventors and marketers of such 'widgets', or 'New Age' thinking, but I think you will know the sort of thing I am talking about. To my mind, the real path to success lies in common sense, patience and kindness. Substitutes for these three things can't be purchased over the counter. Several years ago a new artist's brush was advertised and students in particular saw it as a kind of magic tool that would elevate their work far beyond the ordinary. Of course it didn't, as hard work and in-built talent are needed to produce a painting of quality. I would advocate a strong dose of common sense

The Emperor's New Clothes

In the dog training world there is an overdeveloped penchant for abdicating from or renouncing common sense in favour of a meaningless catchphrase or attractive buzzword. The truth of the matter is simple and consistent and resides in this question: How can I make things better for my dog? Unlike people, the dog will not take advantage of your new-found meekness.

Grooming is one of the most powerful yet gentle tools the dog owner has in the love-your-dog-as-you-love-yourself philosophy.

I can hear some of you saying, 'Oh, come now, don't be daft! This is too simple.' It is simple. But if you commit to doing it every day it takes time, effort, commitment and the application of that rare but precious commodity – common sense.

If I were to draw up a list of the most important things you need to do for your dog I would put grooming just slightly behind exercise, food and warmth as an essential requirement for the wellbeing of that precious creature called dog.

It is a direct and readily understood communication with your dog that tells it conclusively that it is important in your life. Just as you need to know that from the people who are dear to you, so it is equally important to your dog and the older it gets the truer that becomes.

For a rescue or nervous dog, grooming underlines a statement of enormous importance: 'Things are much better here than they used to be in my other place.'

Nothing in the world will convince your new dog that this really is a good place quicker.

I explain myself, here, for all of the faddists and, speaking from my background of twenty years as a professional dog trainer, with I hope some force.

Your dog is much more likely to progress quickly from nervous and unsure rescue dog if:

- It is comfortable

- It is reassured by a regular, practical demonstration of your affection

- It regularly receives one-to-one attention from you

- You are close enough often enough to notice bumps, lumps, bruises and strains or some developing behavioural problem

- You demonstrate that it is more important than the other things you spend time on, such as the love for inanimate, non-love-returning nonsenses that we elevate to a position of unjustified importance

- You enable sufficient close-contact time to learn about your dog and for it to learn about you

You are much more likely to achieve a quickly resettled rescue dog if:

- The lost stranger that has little faith in humans is shown care – not now and again but every day

- What you do with comb and brush soothes away your dog's worries and concerns as well as making its skin and coat comfortable

- You produce a reliable and stable daily reminder of your special relationship

- You actually take time off from more important matters to form a bond with your dog

Have you ever not washed your hair when it really needed it and spent the evening scratching an itchy head? Now, just extend that itching to your whole body and magnify the irritation. Leave that discomfort for weeks, or even months, knit in a few serious tangles of dead hair and ask yourself how you would feel.

Put this into perspective and imagine that you are a nervous dog that receives declarations of undying love but no demonstration of it whatsoever. Then ask yourself a question, will you give of your best? The answer undoubtedly is No!

Show You Care

When I was working in Devon as a shepherd I would see countless sheepdogs running around with coats that had never seen a brush. Their bellies were caked solid with the 'cement' of hard, dried mud and during moulting there were great clumps of dead hair covering their backs. No doubt there were also prickly grass seeds and pieces of sharp bramble woven into their tangled coats as well.

Some farmers would regard their working dogs as tools and would argue that they do not have time to waste grooming them, yet their tractor always has oil and diesel and the tyres and brakes are attended to with great regularity. A bit like lavishing hours each week on a depreciating lump of metal called a car. This is strange to my way of thinking: they have chosen to lavish care on a machine – inanimate and without feelings – while leaving the best friend and helpmate they have ever had in a deplorable state.

Whenever I do sheepdog demonstrations at country shows members of the audience always make these two remarks about the dogs more often than they make any other: 'Don't they look lovely and clean!' 'They really seem to be enjoying themselves.'

There never seems to be an awareness that the two factors are in any way connected.

I have fourteen sheepdogs now but had even more of them when I was doing a show every day. They worked often in extremely muddy conditions but I always found the time to spend on thorough grooming.

I still groom them, at length, every single day and the benefits to them – and in calming me – are enormous. It is a good period and although we know each other inside out it always renews and strengthens the bond between us. Such a simple thing, yet it can yield such a great harvest of benefits.

To my mind grooming is, as I've said, of paramount importance – and even more so if your dog is going to live in the house.

I firmly believe that my dogs have been better performers because of the grooming sessions and that special sort of bonding that has grown because of it.

I am absolutely certain that the quiet times, grooming, being so close to my dogs has improved the way they work for me as well as the more understanding way that I work for them.

Apart from the tangible benefits there is of course the enormous pleasure of spending such quality time in their company.

Grooming also offers an excellent chance to look at the dog every day and to assess its state of health, both physical and mental. It provides an opportunity to check for fleas or ticks and to monitor skin condition. It even makes a silent comment on the benefits of the food and exercise you are giving your dog by the glossy (or otherwise) condition of its fur and the degree of muscle tone and fat you can feel.

Good Grooming

You will not need lots of equipment; I use a brush, a comb with metal tines (teeth) and a pair of scissors, as well as a glove with little raised rubber pads that is excellent for taking off dead hairs.

I use the brush to free the coat of tangles and the fine-toothed comb to take out the dead hair that lies just under the outer coat. The scissors are used to snip off hair that tends to grow too long on the trousers or skirts of my Border collies, or those matted bits that try to hide behind their ears.

If you are rough and try to force your way through tangles the grooming will do more for distancing than bonding so do it as carefully and considerately as you would brushing your own hair. My dogs queue up for their turn so I know that I am doing the job gently and correctly.

It is worth talking to a breed expert or someone who owns the same type of dog as you have as they will know the best way of grooming that breed.

The one thing that I wish I had done is got the dogs used to a hairdryer. When we come back from a particularly wet walk I still dry off each one with a towel which is not the most efficient way to dry as many dogs as I have.

Years ago I did a lecture tour of the East Coast of America, supported by British dog magazines and which I paid for by writing articles for them. I stayed with a Princeton University professor who had two Hungarian Komondors (*Komondorok* in Hungarian), which were originally used to protect flocks of sheep. The dogs have long, corded fur that looks rather like a mop head or dreadlocks so normal drying would be out of the question. The professor had a room fitted out especially for the purpose and used what looked like a large commercial hairdryer to dry his two exceptionally large, long-coated dogs and the whole job was done effortlessly in no time at all.

Somehow I can't see my collies sitting unperturbed while I buzz around them with a noisy hairdryer. If I had my time again, though, I would get them used to it as not only does it dry (with lovely warm air) but is perfect for untangling their fur.

Grooming a Rescue Dog

With a newly acquired rescue dog I would approach the whole task of grooming with some caution. Once again, try to see things from the point of view of your dog. Try to put yourself in its place.

It is unsettled because this is not its first home. It does not know you and might well be both suspicious and nervous about your intentions, especially if you approach the grooming the wrong way.

Initially, instead of the procedure being soothing it could turn out to be stressful.

I have said earlier that too many cuddles too early is not a good idea and, as grooming is a similar action to cuddling, less is more to begin with.

If your new dog is extremely nervous don't rush straight into it but put the brush down on the floor and let your dog sniff it and be comfortable with the object itself. Then pick the brush up and put it down several times, making sure that your movements are steady and smooth. Each picking up and putting down is a chance to find out where you should be standing to put the dog at its ease.

After the dog had been living with me for a week or so I might try a brief brushing, but would stop as soon as I saw any sign of uncertainty in my dog.

I kneel down to groom my dogs but they are used to me and, even now, with some of them, looking straight into their eyes makes them uncomfortable. When you kneel to groom your dog your heads tend to be at the same level and that makes direct eye contact much more likely.

If I thought it safe I would kneel down so that I was not looming over my dog, but I would not look it directly in the eye – that level of trust can come much later on in the relationship.

Being alongside the dog is probably the best position; within the dog's sight line but not staring straight into its eyes.

When you start to actually groom begin with a couple of very soft brush strokes then stop. Each day, double the number of strokes until you end up giving the dog a full ration by which time it should be beginning to enjoy the attention.

If you come across a tangle leave it until the dog is totally at ease with the knowledge that nothing unpleasant or unexpected is going to happen.

Don't for one moment think that because a brush and comb are totally acceptable that the dog will view scissors with the same equanimity. Scissors might well be viewed with some fear as they make a strange clicking sound and cut bits of hair off. Keep the points well away, or better still use scissors with rounded ends. It does not take much to make the dog jump during these early stages and their direction is often straight toward the scissors.

Do take extra care to make sure that what you are cutting is fur. That might sound like a very silly thing to say but I have come close to including a tiny bit of skin with the hair behind the ear and just one misadventure like this could put the progress of trust back where it started.

Once your dog is used to the grooming event being a regular happening you will start to see what a wonderfully calming effect it has and will see why I have made such a fuss about it and singled it out as a major contribution toward the happiness and contentment of your dog.

Now is the time to get your dog used to the fact that it is going to get cuddled. To begin with, sneak the odd cuddle in with the grooming. But do it as though you are merely finding a more suitable position to groom from rather than going for a full frontal, overt cuddle.

A Panacea for Many Ills

My dog Fadey does not see as well as she used to. I suspect it might be more severe than I am prepared to face up to. Whenever Maureen tells me that it is a particular dog's birthday she always adds, '. . . just a young dog'. She knows how inadequate I am at facing reality head on, especially when it comes to my beloved dogs.

Grooming helps Fadey more than even I – huge fan that I am – would have thought possible. It tells her that I am there and that I love her and that everything is still where it used to be: nothing has changed. It is an enormous reassurance and banishes fear most effectively.

I often choose to groom her when she is going to bed because it relaxes her and paves the way for a good sleep.

Grooming can also be employed as a very useful distraction and I have used it with dogs that are frightened of going on a lead or of some other situation.

With a dog that's got a fear of the lead I clip the lead on to the collar but do not take hold of it. Instead, I let it lie with its handle loop on the ground, then I groom the dog for five minutes before picking up the lead.

With a dog that is nervous outside the house, especially one that tends to bark at every person that walks by, you can use grooming as a means of showing the dog that there is nothing untoward or dangerous about the front garden and the disturbing fact that strangers will keep walking past. Take the brush, comb and your dog outside with you and groom in the garden. Gradually the dog will become used to passing strangers and see the whole situation as much more normal.

Grooming sends a message to your dog.
And the message reads: Everything
is as it is meant to be.

Use the grooming process strategically, in clever and useful ways: it is more than just brushing a dog, it is a panacea for many ills.

Make yourself an expert in the art of grooming – the dividends for both you and your best friend will be beyond your most optimistic expectations.

Rescue dogs, once settled, return love
with a passion because they know that they
were once lost but now have been found.

When you are training a dog, the obvious thing to do often does not work as well as you hoped it would; equally, something that you might have considered an unimportant side issue yields benefits way beyond expectations. Grooming is one of those big surprises.

Chapter Fourteen

Ceri's Magic Button

A fox got our Khaki Campbell ducks one black, cold night during the winter. When I went to put them to bed they were lying around their yard like muddy, still parcels, a sight I really did not want to see. It was a blow to me but even more so to Maureen who really loved them to bits.

The ducks had worked with me at the theme park in the indoor arena where they were herded by two gentle dogs. When they came to the end of their working life I made a promise that their retirement would be good – and I hoped it would also be long. Until the fox came along, their retirement had, indeed been good, but this was not the peaceful end I'd had in mind for our Khaki Campbells.

After the anger had subsided a little, I reasoned that Mr Fox doesn't really have much choice about who he is and how he lives – he does what he must.

Later, I reinforced the run to a Fort Knox-like standard putting on a roof as strong as the walls and, after a decent interval, we bought a flock of Aylesbury ducks.

I was conscious of and guilty about closing the stable door after the horse had bolted – how easy it is to be wise after the event.

The Aylesbury ducks are exuberant eating machines. They will mow you down in their enthusiasm to get at their layers pellets when they are let out in the morning. Not shy and nervous like the Campbells these ducks are outgoing, wing-flapping, water-splashing, last-one-in-the-pond's-a-sissy extroverts.

Don't worry, I am not about to set off in praise of white ducks (though they are little dears).

Halfway through Ceri's second month of training I took all my dogs for their customary last walk before bed and then counted them back into their kennels . . . Except that I must have counted someone twice.

My evening is filled with duties, so not much chance to sit back on the sofa and watch television. An hour or so after I'd counted in the dogs, I put the ducks to bed in their houses and then an hour after that I began the longer routine of settling down my fourteen dogs.

As you know, I spend time with each one to make sure that they are comfortable and that they are where they want to be. Bob is old so his settling in time lasts much longer than the others. Muppet, you will recall, may decide to sleep between hay bales under the lean-to rather than in any of his other three places and Megan has to be looked for as the variety of her sleeping places defy my imagination.

Eventually, with all my dogs put to bed I was securing the last padlock when I heard a bark that did not sound as if it was coming from the right place. It was a little more distant, more an echo than a bark.

I had to listen a couple of times before I realised that it was coming from the field behind the kennels. Someone else's dog perhaps? It sounded suspiciously like master Ceri . . . No, that could not be. Couldn't be mine.

Well, it was mine. Somehow, master Ceri had escaped the kennel booking in ritual and had spent two hours or so doing as he pleased. I ought to teach them to respond to my calling out a register:

'Gemma?'

'Here, sir.'

But Border collies are so crafty they would still engineer the situation to suit themselves.

I ought to tell you about the land behind the kennels so you can fully appreciate Ceri's opportunities for mischief.

There is a small home pasture complete with my old show caravan emblazoned with the words 'Sssh Sheepdogs Sleeping'. To the right of the caravan are our ducks and to the right of them the dark forest that borders the fields. To the caravan's left is the orchard with some sheep in it. At the end of the home pasture a twelve-foot, steel farm gate leads to the training field and below that lies a field originally called 'Rick field' – years ago hay stacks stood in it – which is also used for sheep grazing. So, master Ceri of the pricked ears and ever watchful eyes had free run of several fields along with à la carte temptations: rabbits to chase and pheasants to scare witless as well as our Aylesbury ducks and the sheep to draw his hypnotised gaze, the latter two species thankfully now safely protected by sturdy, collie- and fox-proof fencing.

I make light of it now but at the time I was very concerned about what superfluity of naughtiness a dog with time on his paws might be tempted to get up to.

O ye of little faith, there was no need to be so worried because the only question in Ceri's mind had been whether to put his 'fluence on the ducks or the sheep. He had chosen the ducks and a flattened patch of shrubbery bore witness to the length of time he had stared at them, as well as how still he had stayed while he did it. The ducks would have been totally unconcerned – they were long used to the fact that several times a day fourteen Border collies would pass their run like an express train that doesn't stop at their station.

When Ceri reluctantly dawdled back like a naughty schoolboy I was both cross and pleased. I was not cross with Ceri but at myself for not 'counting him in' and I was pleased to find Ceri so trustworthy, that he had contented himself with just looking. This new knowledge of Ceri impressed me.

The 'Eye'

In chapter twelve I wrote that when a dog gets into mischief it can turn from a problem into something beneficial. In this case, I had learned that Ceri, despite his bad beginnings, was the very best kind of sheepdog in that he would look rather than chase. However long he took to look.

Shepherds call this weapon, or tendency, the 'eye'. Some dogs have too much of it and can actually hypnotise themselves by staring too intensely. I have known novice sheepdogs to stand in the middle of a field and stare both the sheep and themselves into statue-like immobility.

So, what could have had a much worse outcome turned out with no harm done and the bonus of knowledge that would inform my training. The ducks will now have another job – to coax out of Ceri what sheepdogs do naturally.

This next stage in his training is quite difficult because I have to teach him two things: that it is actually a good thing for him to watch the ducks and that he should watch them when I tell him rather than when he thinks that it is a good thing to do.

The outcome I am looking for is that when I tell him to move away from the ducks he'll do so immediately and that he will regard it purely as a functional instruction, not as a telling off. When I then tell him to watch the ducks again, he should return immediately to do so.

If I am really clever I can squeeze two more manoeuvres out of this situation: I can ask him to leave by moving to his left or to exit right.

So, a wonderful opportunity has arisen which will enable

me to extract four movements each of which, I hope, will be much more keenly executed by the dog because he will be able to see why I am asking him to do them.

> *I had found something that will motivate Ceri.*
> *I found his 'magic button'.*

Not recognising a dog's natural, breed-induced inclination and treating it instead as something deserving of a telling-off rather than an opportunity can lead to a quick and sometimes hard-to-reverse failure.

Tread Lightly

I remember how seven years ago I was too firm with Sally's sister, Khuni, when she was a young trainee sheepdog and spoiled her future endeavours. It was her first introduction to a flock of sheep and without thinking I had chosen a group of ewes who were in the later stages of pregnancy.

The field was long and narrow and because Khuni runs much faster than I can she arrived on the scene before I had managed to get into a commanding position – mistake number one.

Khuni enthusiastically set about this new and exciting game of driving sheep, except she did it too diligently and would not leave them when I told her to. I had shouted at the top of my voice at her to stop and, eventually, she did. But as a result of my ferocity she never wanted to work them again – mistake number two.

There are key moments in training a dog that can turn all things for bad or for good. It takes great awareness to recognise them. This was a crucial moment!

It is a big mistake to try and suppress an instinct that has taken hundreds, maybe thousands, of years to develop.

The ewes, incidentally, were fine, but you can see that even very experienced trainers sometimes get it completely wrong.

There are two lessons to be learned here. First, your dog will not have your sense of right and wrong and the chances of getting it to assimilate both instruction and criticism at this early stage is most unlikely. Secondly, what appears to be a tough dog can often be a sensitive and easily discouraged one. I had failed to judge Khuni correctly.

Of course, I already knew that I needed to handle Ceri with sensitivity, the problem I faced was that I would need to exert some control in order to achieve our aim in training: to encourage his natural tendency to be a good, attentive sheepdog while at the same time ensuring that he did it when I decided he should, not on his own terms.

If I had just shouted angrily he would certainly have stopped looking at the ducks but he might also have thought that this meant that he should not keenly watch any moving creature from this moment on, which would have resulted in a dog unable to do what he was designed by hundreds of years of careful breeding to do and perhaps some other behavioural problem would be inadvertently caused by the frustration.

Once too firm a block is put on a particular action most dogs will not be able to relearn the process. They will regard your fierce reaction as having meant that they must never again repeat that action (or indeed anything like it) under any circumstances.

If you react in the right way you can use most situations to great advantage and turn something that concerned you into a huge leap forward. So, think about how you deliver any instruction. When we get angry it is not just our voice that communicates with our dog but, more meaningfully, our body language and this is what our dog reads. Your face tensed, eyes narrowed, shoulders up, and as you shout out your head thrust forward – when the dog sees that extreme anger it might be so overwhelmed that it doesn't even hear your words. Communicate an unintended message in anger and you may instil extreme fear into the mind of your dog which may recur in the dog when it's faced with the same, or a similar situation in the future.

If you are tempted to shout in a tricky situation resist it unless you are insisting that your dog comes back from a potentially dangerous situation.

Don't make judgements on the spur of the moment. If you can't be clear in your own mind then your dog will have no chance of sorting it out in theirs.

My considered advice would always be to take a thoughtful approach to training; be patient and you will reap the benefits in the long term.

Make the Most of What You Have to Work With

It is always going to be much easier to get a dog to do something it is interested in doing than something it does not want to do. An example would be with a dog that would rather stand than sit – the objective is to get the dog to stop so, whether it wants to stand or sit when it stops is neither here nor there.

I put Ceri to bed with a pat, told him 'good boy', and resisted all temptation to chastise him.

As I walked back to the house I thought carefully and calmly about the direction I should take with his training. I thought long and hard about how to achieve our objective: I wanted to encourage Ceri to come away from the ducks when I told him without lessening or damaging the urge that drove him there in the first place; equally, I wanted to position him to watch the ducks as though both 'watch' and 'leave' were my intentional inventions rather than just a reaction to his compulsion. By the next morning I had figured out the best way.

A dog will never realise that it decided on a course of action rather than you choosing it. Ceri will simply see this as something he got right first time and that will add more willingness and confidence to what he does in the future.

I started that morning, first, by leading him to the side of the duck enclosure and telling him to 'lie down' – I'd noticed that he lay down anyway so, there would be a bonus to keeping to that. After ten minutes or so I used the word 'here' to lead him away from the ducks. Over the next month I shall vary the time between the two commands so that he believes that he is doing what I want him to do. Why should

I bother with such a complicated procedure? Because I will have managed to get Ceri to treat both 'lie down' and 'here' in a matter-of-fact way that does not damage his natural inclination, which means I can use both commands in any other situation that demands them.

Rather than have to teach him to 'lie down' as an isolated exercise, his understanding of and response to that command will have been achieved naturally.

When I was training Annie, my first Border collie, I used 'tibs' – Devon dialect for lambs – as a 'situation' command. What I mean by that is that her reaction to it would depend on the situation: if the ewes had just had lambs, on the command 'tibs' she would go around the field to check that the lambs were all all right; when she was faced with a mass of sheep and lambs in a country lane 'tibs' would get her to move them along the lane in the direction my body language indicated.

Always remember, the dog reads the body language first and takes notice of the command second. Body language will always be the best means of communicating.

You can use the same word said fiercely, questioningly, softly or loudly and your dog will, after training, be able to understand what the tone variation means.

So Ceri, instead of feeling that I am mightily displeased if I were to bellow 'COME AWAY', will react as though it is all in a day's work. This way, the instruction will not damage or inhibit Ceri but encourage him to respond immediately.

Duck-sitter in Training

Next day, I took the ducks out for a walk – without master Ceri – to see how they moved and what sort of speed suited them best.

I think that I will be able to teach Ceri to look after them gently.

Foxes, even in daylight, are always looking for their next meal but with a very protective and determined Ceri acting as the ducks' ever-present minder, the fox would need his head tested to venture too near.

If it works I shall, with great joy, reveal all; if it doesn't I shall still include all but with a little less enthusiasm.

Things do not always go according to plan but I think my assessment of Ceri's potential is an accurate one. So, do not worry about the ducks as they will be in very safe paws.

Chapter Fifteen

Galleons under Full Sail

I let the Aylesbury ducks out for the first time on one of the hottest days this year. They needed no cajoling – all I had to do was to open the door of their yard and they bundled their way out like ladies who have been waiting for a sale to open. They pushed through their yard gate on to the cool and very lush grass in what seemed like seconds.

My plan was to delay bringing Ceri out until the end of their hopefully enjoyable experience of freedom. I have never seen such joy. Aylesbury ducks riffle through long grass at amazing speed. At first I thought they were eating it but soon noticed that they were in effect filtering the grass, just in case some juicy morsel such as an unsuspecting slug was sunbathing on one of the long stems. Judging by the ducks' enthusiasm the grass must have been like Brighton beach, in a slug sense.

A Duck to Train Your Dog?

As I said, the ducks we lost to the fox were Khaki Campbells. Their upright body shape reminds me of a meerkat standing up on its hind legs, and the Campbells – which carry far less body weight than Aylesburys – can move very quickly. Ducks with an upright shape are runners – most either can't or can only barely fly – while those with a horizontal shape fly. As a breed, Aylesbury ducks are a little too like huge troop carriers to fly more than a few feet – ours can't actually get off the ground and they do not walk very quickly, either.

At the Milky Way theme park I used our Khaki Campbells as substitute sheep and the duck trial in the indoor arena was hugely popular.

Mollie and Bob worked the ducks and over the course of a couple of months' practice became impressively adept at herding them through a couple of miniature farm gates, a tunnel, up a ramp and into a pond.

Some of the staff at the park built a miniature pub for me to use in the duck trial, complete with windows and a hinged front door. I thatched the roof and made a swinging sign then painted 'The Duck Inn' on it. At the beginning of the show I would open the door and a host of ducks would dash out accompanied by much loud and prolonged laughter, especially from the children in the audience.

I had trained Mollie and Bob on the much heavier, slower moving and truly stubborn Muscovy duck. Muscovies do not waste their time being intimidated by dogs and it is a real achievement to actually move them. Their stubborn ways and snail-slow walking speed render them perfect for training dogs. Nothing alarms the distinctively red-faced Muscovy and the males are not slow to give a dog that comes too close a good nip.

My training theory was a little like that of a middle distance runner training on sand in army boots: if I could learn to cope with the very worst, the best would seem easy.

The Muscovies had certainly helped me to train my dogs to herd ducks both gently and to great effect. As my Aylesbury ducks seem similar in speed and temperament they might just benefit Ceri's education in the same way. We shall see.

I was so fascinated by the ducks' antics, their obvious enjoyment and their compulsion to rummage energetically through every patch of grass they found, that I found I had unintentionally extended their exercise period to over two hours. Sitting in the sun and watching these entertaining creatures just gobbled up the time as effectively as they were gobbling up the grass.

I could hear by his barks from the yard and the fact that all of the other dogs were quiet that Ceri had some sort of inkling that all of this carry-on might have something to do with him.

In some ways, basing what I saw of his habit of lying down next to their pen for as long as I would allow him to do it, I think that Ceri may have felt that the ducks belonged to him.

However confident I might feel about Ceri's impending performance I had taken the precaution of bringing one of my shepherd's crooks out with me. I'd made sure that it was not one of my best show sticks as I remembered how Misty (who did not want to work ducks) had shown her displeasure by biting lumps off the end of a previous one. It had started life at a respectable five-feet and been whittled down by naughty Misty to an unusable three-feet.

My shepherd's crook tells my dogs that real work is pending and that I am taking it seriously in the same way that, when I was a vicar, my best suit would tell them that Sunday was not a working day – well, not for them anyway.

Crooks are useful in that the handle at the end fits nicely, and comfortably, around the dog's neck so, if it becomes over-excited and doesn't listen to what it's being told its enthusiasm can be gently but firmly arrested, even (and especially) when the dog is beyond arm's length. Better, I reasoned, a momentarily discontented dog than an over-harried duck.

Dogs are always surprised when they discover that you can still reach them even though they think that they are too far away from you and therefore free to do whatever they fancy doing.

If you can surprise them with an extendable reach they will never, unless they are extremely intelligent, underestimate you again.

Bob was wise to the 'extendable reach' principle when herding very large, strong Embden geese and very able at defending themselves. In an attempt to encourage Bob to come closer so that they could peck him, the geese would try to bamboozle him by 'winding' in their necks to half their true length. Bob would respond by drawing his head unnaturally close to his body to suggest that his neck, and reach, were much shorter than they were.

The double bluff always worked in Bob's favour – the geese always underestimated his extendable reach. Geese are extremely intelligent in every other regard and I can remember them showing real annoyance and surprise that they had been out-thought yet again.

Peck, incidentally, is the most understated word when related to a goose. What they actually do is find the softest part of the victim's body, for which they have an uncannily accurate grasp combined with a crack bomber's ability to hit their target, and with their serrated beaks they turn, twist and grip the loose skin to produce a pinch that certainly makes the eyes water.

Ceri Meets the Ducks

So, crook (useful arm extension) in hand, I prepared to let Ceri out. This would be a real acid test of his personality and a guide to what might follow in the way of further training. Though I use a discernible training method I am always prepared to be flexible and adapt it in line with each different dog's needs.

Well, Ceri came out and rushed like mad to his usual spot up against the wire fence of the duck yard. He looked intently through the wire but there was not a duck in sight. He did not seem too disturbed by this discovery but, there again, he could probably hear – and would certainly have scented – that they were nearby.

When Ceri did notice the ducks he looked surprised to see them on the 'wrong' side of their enclosure. He looked me full in the face and then at the Aylesburys. Then he repeated his response to the surprise he'd had when he heard my voice on the hand-held tape recorder: he weighed it all up very quickly and got on with his business.

The trouble was he obviously believed that his job was to just lie down and watch the ducks. No notice was taken of my spoken commands, though I tried several times to get him up on his feet.

What Ceri did take notice of was my movement. If I walked to my right he would move to his, in order to establish a balance.

The ducks waddling around between us made quick decisions about which of us might be the most dangerous and plumped for Ceri (good choice). So, as I walked backward they moved toward me and, after a brief hesitation Ceri got up on his feet and moved toward the ducks. I kept an eagle eye on him all the time in case herding should turn into something else, but it didn't.

The process had begun. It was happening as it should. The ducks were moving by default yet it would, I hoped, appear to Ceri that they were moving under his influence. If they moved he would respond by moving too.

Although the outcome of this first test is most pleasing I did note that Ceri does not, as yet, quite understand the objective in that he, eventually, will be expected to move the ducks rather respond to their movement.

He obviously regards his role to be a guardian rather than a mover. I am pleased, though, as this is an excellent first result and a guard is much better than a chaser. It would be unreasonable to expect him to look forward to the next step, as that is a human construct.

It will not take too many sessions before I have made Ceri good enough to look after the ducks in the orchard but that can wait, we have time.

Enjoyment, Training and Reward: The Perfect Package

I am fully aware that your desire, or need, to move ducks around probably does not rate highly on your most wanted list. The point of all of this is to show that I have taken into account what type of dog Ceri is and I know from experience that training is always made much easier by using the right motivational tools.

Border collies herd, so herding will (in Ceri's case) make learning easier. As he learns, progressive success will go hand in hand with his contentment which will, in turn, improve his behaviour.

The same principle applies to gun dogs. If you employ a training method that suits their disposition you will achieve far better results than using a training form alien to their nature. So, for example, throw a dummy and get the dog to find it and bring it back to you.

I have a friend who is a dog behaviour therapist and who, very cleverly, motivated her dogs using a device that was much more imaginative than the standard treat bribe that I so disagree with. She made her dogs work for their reward by doing what a dog does naturally, as well as using the device as a training aid.

She cut raw liver into slivers then hid them some way away from her dogs. She directed the dogs to track down the pieces of liver by using the same body language signals she used with them in everyday training.

They loved tracking it and, of course, found the liver and were thus rewarded for their efforts all in one enjoyable episode. That is clever! Those dogs would look forward to their next tracking lesson and be learning at twice the speed because my friend was using a motivational device linked to what the dogs would do naturally.

> *Enjoyment, training and reward all wrapped up into one intelligent package.*

So, if you want to sharpen up your dog's interest in training try hiding a small piece of liver and then directing your dog's efforts by the use of commands such as 'here' and body language signals especially the use of the arms as pointers.

This will have a dramatic effect on a dog that gives every impression of having no interest in training sessions. The second time the liver hiding happens you will find that you suddenly have the most attentive dog in the world. A note of caution: dogs are not good at knowing where the liver slices end and the fingers begin.

If, for example, your dog is not interested in chasing a ball or a Frisbee smear a little liver juice on it and watch the interest increase. But don't rush out and buy huge amounts of liver as this tool comes very much under the 'use rarely' heading.

The point of all this is that your progress in training a rescue or nervous dog will be made so much quicker and much more enjoyable the moment you realise that your dog is motivated by doing what it likes doing.

> *Very few dogs will be interested in training for its own sake.*

Read a book about your dog's breed and the breed's purpose and then tailor the training to fit that. If your dog is not a pure breed, or you are uncertain what it might be, then observe the dog in order to work out what it likes and what it dislikes and try to make the training fit within its likes.

> *Work with your dog not against it!*

Finding Jack's Problem: Month Two

When a dog does what its breeding intended it to do the training is much easier because it is predictable. Any breed book will give you a fair indication of what to expect and thereby save you an awful lot of experimentation time.

Jack, as I have already said, is nervous – whether he has always been so or whether something we have done has caused his nervousness, I have no way of knowing.

> *Just as there are nervous people, there are naturally nervous dogs.*

When a Border collie does what it is meant to do, finding something that will motivate it is straightforward. When it does not fit the expected pattern of behaviour in a working context the natural process is prevented from happening by the dog's lack of interest.

More time is spent looking for signs that might tell you what the problem is rather than actually doing anything about it.

Now two months into Jack's training I was lucky enough to get a clue this week thanks to my female dogs coming into season. At the beginning, when I first notice that it is about to happen I continue to allow all the dogs to go out together but as the effects of their seasons become less controllable – by dint of galloping hormones – I separate the sexes.

It was during the extreme nagging period ('come away Ben, and you Barney!') just before the raging hormones made life and control just too difficult that I pinned down Jack's problem.

Jack takes all the blame upon himself.

Even though the name I am shouting is not Jack's, even though I am not looking at him, the effect on him is dramatic while the dog I am shouting at is made of sterner stuff and takes little notice. A couple of times I'd had to shout to some of the dogs – though not Jack – to 'come away' from one of the bitches, and on both occasions Jack took himself off home to his kennel to get some peace in a place he obviously considers safe.

The next morning he did not even come out to join us. He, wisely, knew that there was little point and that the first shout would send him back to his kennel. Now that I have seen this I realise that there is no value in normal training. Anything that looks like a demand is going to put him off before we even start.

Sheepdogs are usually subject to an irresistible compulsion to work whereas Jack regards work as the very thing that brings on stressful situations.

> *While Ceri's problems can be cured by encouraging him to lose himself in work any sign that work might be on my agenda will send Jack into paroxysms of anxiety.*

This fear swamps Jack and completely overcomes him. It will make his training exceedingly difficult because I shall have to camouflage the work to look like a game and if he recognises the ulterior motive then all will be lost. Dogs have good memories so if I succeed in making work look like something else but then he sees through it, yet another barrier will have been erected in Jack's already fragile and suspicious mind.

For the moment, I must confess to being almost as confused as Jack is and whenever this happens I always do the same thing: we shall go out on our own to a peaceful place.

I shall look at him all over again in the hope that I might just discover what is causing his underlying fears and think, again, how I can motivate him sufficiently to be bothered to go some way toward responding to my overtures.

So far, I have spent two months on Jack and achieved very little indeed. In the same time Ceri has learned to perform at least six actions promptly and stylishly.

I shall persist.

Chapter Sixteen

Tender Jack

The more I look at Jack and observe his behaviour the more clearly I notice that, as I have noted before, he is very vulnerable and much too tender.

If there is any kind of fracas, or even if it appears that there might be, Jack vanishes from the location of the disturbance and hides himself away in his safe kennel. If I quickly look to the right at Barney then immediately glance back to where Jack was – no Jack!

It is not just a reaction but a statement of his unease.

The only good thing to emerge from all of this is that at last he does regard his kennel as safe. There is at least an always available bolt hole deemed by him to be safe and that alone is progress.

If in the middle of a walk in the park your dog suddenly vanishes it might well be that loud and harsh words preceded its disappearance, rather than that it is simply misbehaving.

Stress in our pack is at its greatest when the girls are in season and there is aggravation from both male and female dogs as well as from the humans who are intent on avoiding misadventures between amorous suitors. And the otherwise banished, loud human voice sneaks back into territory that it has been excluded from because a shouted command is the only way to distract two passionate dogs from repopulating the earth with their progeny.

Jack likes all things to be calm (and, for that matter, so do I).

The Key to Training Jack: Month Three

At last I have figured out how to train Jack. My aim is not only to make him better at routine functions such as to 'come' or 'sit' but also – and much more importantly for him – to make him feel at ease and to stop believing that harsh words intended for another individual have something to do with him.

I want, in short, to set him free from his fears and make him happier. Achieving perfection in his work comes a lot lower down my list of priorities than does achieving his contentment. After all, if I cannot make him happy and at ease there will be no chance of achieving much with his training.

Jack is worried about anything that looks intense or demanding. I shall, therefore, disguise any session we have so that it looks like an undemanding stroll around the fields.

If there is one thing he really enjoys it is to be outdoors on his own with me when it is obvious that work is not on the agenda and the pace of all things is leisurely.

Let's Pretend . . .

I began the game of great pretence by carrying a rake rather than a crook, as though my purpose was to pile up grass that had been scythed the previous day. Thus, from Jack's point of view, I was not going to be putting my trainer's intent eye on him nor did it look likely that I would be expecting anything from him beyond a nice walk around a very pleasant field.

It is surprising that a dog can recognise the difference between a rake and a shepherd's crook. Perhaps it's the difference in the bearer's attitude that puts them at ease rather than the shape of the tool.

Jack set off with me with what looked very much like a smile on his lips and we headed for a sheep field – one that is not used for dog training.

And that was my second ploy in this game of pretend.

Jack's body language certainly indicated that he was very relaxed about the whole thing. I did start to rake the grass but, now and again, whistled softly and up he came, every time, as instantly as is possible.

The day before, I had realised that spoken commands faze Jack – because their content is specific and tell him clearly that what is about to happen is going to be too demanding to be enjoyable.

Each time I whistled I used exactly the same signal and every time he responded in a joyful and willing way. Usually, 'joyful' and 'willing' would be the very last words that could be attached to Jack's demeanour. Real progress was at last being made.

I did not want to do too much on the first day in case his old fears crept back and spoiled our progress. I did, however, add in a couple of different whistles accompanied by hand and arm signals that indicated that I was going to the left or right and that I would rather like him to come with me. And, yes, on the very first command he came back bringing a wagging tail behind him.

The subterfuge had worked brilliantly and at no time did any sort of suspicion rise in Jack's mind. Whenever I bent down to pull grass out of the tines of my rake he came over to see me, recognising that bent knees represent a cuddling opportunity.

We were out for around one and-a-half hours and my profit was twofold: I had a big pile of grass drying in the field and, much more to the point, Jack, the impenetrable, had begun to show me a little of his true nature.

On our way back from the grass field I let the ducks out to see if this session had reawakened any of Jack's natural sheepdog instincts. It had not! He strolled up to see what these feathered creatures were doing outside their pen (and in totally the wrong place) but his interest was short-lived and he soon returned to his doggy, field-sniffing duties.

Avoid Preconceptions

'I have never met a dog that could not be trained once the right approach is found.' That quote from my first book is central to my beliefs. I referred to it earlier, here, when I first described Jack and said that he would test it to its limit.

Well, even though finding the right approach to Jack was more difficult than finding a needle in a haystack, I think it has been found and now I should be able to progress. I no longer need to keep doubling back in the hope of finding something that would work, checking and rechecking to see if I had missed something important.

Jack, though he is a sheepdog, actually isn't one when it comes to tendency or application. None of that restless compulsion to work is in him.

Jack is quite simply 'a dog' and the quicker
my expectations exclude anything to do
with task-training a typical sheepdog the
better everything will be.

There's a lesson here: when we have expectations of how a dog should be, but the dog does not behave as we expect, the resulting disappointment we feel can show enough for the dog to notice our change in attitude toward it and become inhibited.

When I give talks or hold clinics one of the most frequent problems I am presented with is from owners of two or more dogs: one will be, they tell me, 'good', the other 'not so good'. The dog that responds instantly to commands is cuddled whereas the one that is frightened by the command (whoever it was addressed to) is not.

I think the dog that is 'not so good' receives far less praise, pats and cuddles than the dog who is 'good' and, of course, the under-achieving dog doesn't see this as any kind of performance-related response but as a sign of being loved less. From the moment it realises that it is not as valued as the 'good' dog, its behaviour will worsen so that in the end the 'good' dog, 'bad' dog comparison will have some real substance to it. The difference, however, will have been created inadvertently by its owner – though by the time that happens they will have mistakenly put the blame on the dog.

We can make a dog 'good' by training, but we can also make a dog less good by inadequate, misguided or insensitive treatment.

Dogs Can Sense the Degree of Regard We Have for Them

I have often noticed how happy Jack is when he is working with his pack and given how difficult it can be when he is on his own or with fewer dogs I can, now, see why. He can hide himself among the pack and avoid my close scrutiny. Similarly, when he is on his own with me he is happier when my attention is directed toward raking grass or doing some other job on the land because that means he is not under my intense observation.

I dare say the cuddles he gets afterwards must go some way to restoring him as the centre of my attention and can do nothing but good.

Today's training has been most rewarding because, in a sense, I have got my Jack back, in a much more complete way than before.

If you have a dog that behaves like Jack keep looking for the key that will unlock its problems – there will be one, you can be sure of that. When you find it the rewards are really heartening. And once you do find the key, put it somewhere safe and don't forget how to use it.

Jack is an enigma and even though I have found the way to motivate him I will not be surprised if other problems pop up. When I first started to train and write down my experiences with Jack I found it very difficult to find enough to say, but now it looks as though he might provide the most interesting chapters.

Ceri Learns Fast

You will recall when I first started training Ceri that I noticed how wary he was over anything that looked as though it might be intense. A game was just fine, but work? No thank you, we don't do serious work!

You will remember me saying that too firm a grasp on his body or collar intimidated him and that he found lots of fleeting touching much more acceptable because such contact, like a game, did not signify that something demanding was about to happen.

What a difference two months has made. Anything that looks like hard, demanding work is now the most loved part of this hitherto nervous dog's day.

The message Ceri gives me now is, 'Give me more hard work!'

I expected a change, of course, because I have seen before the huge differences between the unsatisfied and the fulfilled Border collie. But such a rapid improvement in both social behaviour and the eagerness to learn is beyond both my experience and wildest expectation.

I would have been delighted to have had a dog of his quality when I earned my living as a demonstrator of dog skills.

To recap: ten-minute training sessions for the first month concentrated on him understanding my body language in order to follow me as I walked in different directions; during the second month the sessions were of the same length but I added voice commands using 'Here' to make it plain that we were going straight on or turning left or right. He was quite good at these manoeuvres but not exceptional.

What made all the difference in the world to Ceri's training regime was recognising, when he lay down by the duck pen and fixed his gaze on them, that he would respond to a real job.

This discovery boosted progress and his hitherto hidden abilities came to the fore in leaps and bounds. During this period the instructions to 'lie down' and 'come here' were learned quickly and cemented firmly in his mind because they were linked with something he *wanted* to do. I have had Ceri out with the ducks three times and he has improved steadily, learning to lie down, walk on and move left and right on command – body language helped because, by now, he understood that he needed to move in the same direction as me.

Hand Signals

If you are concerned about what sort of body movement or hand signal to use do not worry. The important thing is to be consistent and make each signal clear and purposeful – inject a little drama, as it were. The verbal command accompanies the movement so, for example, you would say, 'lie down' while pushing both hands down toward the ground.

The hand signals the police use to direct traffic are a good example of what you are aiming for – larger than life gestures to 'stop', 'go' and 'turn left/right'.

Your dog will more readily understand signals such as these than it will grasp your words. Though communicating instructions using body language may seem foreign to you at first, your dog will find it easier to fathom than verbal commands.

The association with the first use of a body-language signal is not usually made quickly but after many repeats it will be learned and progress will get quicker on subsequent signals because the dog by then understands the currency you are using.

Ceri's progress has been the fastest I have ever seen from all of the many dogs I have trained, except perhaps the canine genius, Bob – like father, like son! With this in mind, do not be disappointed if your dog takes longer to achieve positive results.

With both Jack and Ceri a very thorough
grooming followed every training session.
I could not overstress the importance of this
if I repeated it a dozen times
(and I probably will).

Grooming is all things pleasant. It reassures, says thank you and well done – it is the glue of your relationship. It confirms your love and puts the demands of training in context.

Chapter Seventeen

Ceri and Jack: Month Four

Each time I start a new month's training I re-read my previous chapters to see how much progress we have made. As a little advance is made every day it is quite easy not to notice the improvements made whereas when it is written down the progress is much more obvious.

Now, when I read the chapters written at the beginning of the training I am surprised at how far we have come in such a short space of time. Training regularly not only improves your dog but teaches you all sorts of things about them that would not have been spotted without the focus that training provides.

In the last three months I have found Ceri's 'magic

button' and thus armed have been able to put progress into overdrive. Jack, who has always had obvious problems is now a book I can begin to read (albeit a difficult one) because training him has concentrated my attention on him more deeply than ever before. I have seen new things about him including the very discovery I needed to be able to go forward.

Both dogs had real but quite different problems and the causes were so well hidden that if I had trained them in the style of 'I am your master and you will do as you are told' no progress would have been made. In fact, their problems would have become ingrained and probably insurmountable.

Take bed-wetting in the case of an older child, for example. This may be the manifestation of a hidden fear or anxiety – wetting the bed is the symptom not the cause. It would likely deepen the problem if the parent told the child off for it; there are more sensitive ways to treat the problem.

A managing director I knew used to say, 'Never rely on assumption.' In his *Reflections on the Psalms* (1961), C. S. Lewis put the same point another way: 'Make no assumptions before looking at the evidence.'

Look carefully at your dog before you embark on any course of training and use the evidence of your observations to tailor the training. Assuming anything almost guarantees a wrong conclusion.

No progress can be made until you have divined the problem or problems that hamper your dog, thus you can progress only by observation and understanding.

Ceri Connects Hand and Voice

I carried on improving Ceri's understanding of body language and because working with the ducks had deepened his desire and provided a great motivation, the signs I made could be more understated.

Some explanation is needed here. Ceri, because he is a dog, understands more about body language than I ever will. So what I had in the earlier stages wanted to make clear to him with my very much overstated and exaggerated signals was that we were entering a training routine and I expected him to react to my signals rather than just observe them.

It would be of little use if he understood them but made no connection between the signals and the fact that he was expected to produce the action. Once he firmly understood that principle I could move on to using less flamboyant signals, accompanied by verbal instructions.

I slightly shifted the emphasis so, while still walking ten yards then turning back and stopping – expecting him to follow my actions – I added the word 'turn' and, finally, 'stop' followed by 'lie down'. You will remember I had introduced 'stop' and 'lie down' earlier when he was working with the ducks. Over the course of the fourth month I also gradually ceased to rely on such previously exaggerated, theatrical signals.

All of the sequence was very quickly learned especially the 'stop' and 'lie down' – which he had come across before. The 'turn' signal took longer but when it was accompanied by an exaggerated body movement from me he fairly quickly grasped my meaning. On the 'come' signal progress was rapid to the degree that I did not have to bend my knees and squat in order to make the message clear – I needed only to make a hand movement such as I might signal to another person if I wanted them to come close to me.

I ought to repeat that as long as you consistently use the same signals the meaning of them will soon become clear to your dog.

> *There is no need for a manual of approved hand signals but consistency is vital.*

Just now and again something fortuitous will happen while you are training your dog so you need to keep watching and capitalise on the moment.

An example of what I mean by this is a dog that has difficulty sitting down on command. I remember watching a dog-walker who kept telling their dog to 'sit down' but the dog never took any notice and would continue to stand. The dog-walker got more and more frustrated yet never noticed that every time they stopped for a chat with a neighbour the dog sat down naturally without the hint of a command.

What the dog-walker should have done was talk to neighbours more, and when the dog sat down repeated the command to 'sit down' in a softer voice, even though it was already sitting down, and then praised the dog like mad.

This would have been so much easier and without struggle and frustration and fairly quickly the dog would have grasped the meaning of the instruction without being confused and intimidated.

Jack's Low Self-esteem

Even though Jack has made huge improvements I still do not think that he is ready to progress his training by more normal methods. You will remember that subterfuge was employed in that the only way I could get him to follow any instruction was by pretending that I was raking grass and just talking to him during spare moments. This ploy suggested to Jack that my attention was not ruthlessly on him but elsewhere so would not prove to be frighteningly demanding.

I suspect that I am close to being able to do away with the pretence but am loath to take the risk this early in the procedure lest I put him back where he began.

One of Jack's problems is that he is not able to assess how much I value him. If he could draw up a list of the most loved dogs in my pack I think he would place himself last.

It is not that there is any kind of block that prevents him from receiving loving attention because it is quite obvious that he loves it, the problem is rather that Jack undervalues himself so such an extent that he cannot imagine me wanting to spend time with him. This is not a problem that is shared by any of my other dogs except, in some part, by Ceri.

As I have said before, all my other dogs push themselves to the front of the queue in order to greedily collect as much fuss as they possibly can and their attitude would suggest that the cuddles are their rightful due. In fact, each appears to regard that it, above all others, is most deserving of my attention.

Both Jack and Ceri, though each to a different degree, tend to show some surprise at being chosen for loving attention. It is as if they are saying, 'But I do not deserve this' – or they will look at me with suspicion as though the cuddles are not given as an unreserved gift but have some ulterior motive.

The strange thing is that neither of them show any reluctance whatsoever when food, rather than affection, is being dished out. With food, both show by their body language that they consider it their due.

A similar situation exists in some human families. The favourite child expects preferential treatment whereas one who considers themselves to be on the fringes will have great difficulty accepting affection as a given and, regarding it as abnormal and with suspicion, is never totally comfortable with it.

My ability to explore this line of reasoning is enhanced by the fact that, as a child, I was rather like both Jack and Ceri in that I most certainly could not be regarded as a favourite but more as a difficult child living on the fringe of the social goings-on of my family. I viewed affection in the same way that Jack and Ceri do, always looking for the ulterior motive.

I do not know how tightly I can tie this comparison between dog and human but I do believe that there is merit in pursuing the thought just a little further. I believe that the reason I would have been regarded as 'difficult' by my parents was caused by my failure to meet their expectations. We had different levels of intelligence and my method of thinking had little to do with theirs so there appeared to be no common ground and this resulted in a great wariness between us.

Find the Reason, Find the Cure

Now, humans regard dogs as being similar to children in that they need to be looked after and in as much as they have expectations of their dogs that might or might not coincide with what actually happens. If the dog fails to live up to our expectations we may react by showing open frustration, discontent or, perhaps, some more subtle form of irritation.

The dog, as I explained earlier, has a huge ability to read how we feel by how we behave rather than what we say and will be fully aware that we are not satisfied with it. But, lacking the human power of reason, the dog will not be able to work out why.

If all of this is true, I can blame Ceri's previous owner for Ceri's behaviour but have no one to blame for Jack's disturbing ways but myself.

Your dog may have none of the problems I have talked about, all of them, or a different set altogether. Whatever is the case, I hope my method of thinking shows how far it is sometimes necessary to go in order to discover why your dog does what it does and that knowing the cause of the problem makes it much easier to cure.

Patience Pays Dividends

I continued with my game of pretend with Jack but gradually reduced the grass-raking and increased the instruction. My balancing act between the two had to be very carefully managed to respond whenever Jack appeared troubled that I was showing too intense an interest in the demanding business of training or he felt my focus too much upon him.

Whenever I noticed that familiar, wary look in his eyes I backed off and transferred my concentration to raking the grass.

By the end of the fourth month's training he was responding well and would travel in any direction I wanted him to as well as coming back immediately and lying down on the very first instruction.

At this stage, one of the biggest advances is that Jack has stopped just wandering off and will now stay near me for as long as I want him to.

In the coming month I shall try to drop the overstated pretence that my attention is not on him but if he is unhappy with that I will not persist just because I would prefer to. It is Jack's contentment that I am trying to achieve, rather than my own.

Chapter Eighteen

Month Five: A Review of My Candidates' Training

If I were training a confident Border collie puppy to be a working sheepdog I would have a clear performance target to aim at and firm plans about how to achieve it.

There would be a certain amount of flexibility built in, for I would want to take advantage of observations about the trainee's character so that the training would sensitively fit but I would, nevertheless, know roughly where I was going.

With a nervous dog my attitude would be quite different and with a rescue dog, different again. I would, with both of these types of dog, travel more in hope than expectation.

If a firm plan is made it means that your expectations will be met whatever the effects on your dog.

My consideration in the case of a nervous dog or a rescue dog, would be for the dog rather than its performance.

This is a good place to include a summary of where we began and how far we have travelled.

Ceri: Eureka!

When I started to train Ceri and Jack I described Ceri's outlook on life as though he were speaking it, 'Yes, you are nice to me now, but will it last?' He was deeply suspicious of humans and what they might do next. This would have come about because of the way he was treated by his previous owner.

I thought that it would affect every aspect of his training far more than it actually did and I worried a lot about things that might happen that did not happen.

I had a hunch that he would be motivated by work and that this might push his worries much more into the background of his mind. Once he had demonstrated how strong his desire to work was, and had been allowed to do it, his fears seemed to evaporate. My theory has always been that a dog's fears can be lessened but never completely erased. Time alone will tell me whether this is true for Ceri.

Ceri's progress has been rapid and because of his new-found confidence continues to advance in leaps and bounds.

Now, he no longer sees me as the man whose mood might suddenly change for the worse but, instead, as the supplier of all good things. The mistrust that was there at the start of his training seems, to all intents and purposes, to have gone.

Two things have brought Ceri and me to this much-improved relationship. The first is that work has provided the 'magic button' that motivates him. The second is that everything that has been done in his training has included a soft voice and much patience.

Motivation Is Key

If you own an active dog like Ceri the method of training I have used will be useful to you. The 'magic button' will need to be found and it will more than likely be different to Ceri's.

You might find that a ball, dummy or Frisbee is the thing that motivates and helps speed up your dog's understanding and willingness for the task in hand. It might be hiding small pieces of raw liver in the grass or the bushes of your garden and getting your dog to find it that boosts its interest in the training – but do this at the end of a training session and make it the rare exception rather than a regular thing.

A quick note on effort and reward (or treat) is needed here. Treats are a bad idea because the dog will not make the association between obeying your last command and receiving the reward of a treat. Rewarding the efforts of what a dog would consider irrelevant and abstract tasks will not be appreciated and nothing will be learned from them. Tracking down and finding a 'treat' through its own direct effort is quite another matter and something it will understand because that is something that it would do naturally.

Using the liver-tracking technique on Ceri, for example, would do more harm than good and would prove a distraction from his real treat which is to be allowed to work.

Jack and Ceri: Different Dogs, Different Problems

Jack is totally different from Ceri – for a start, he is not a rescue dog. But, within my broader definition of 'rescue' he did need to be rescued from his problems. I have had him since the minute of his birth and he is most definitely a disturbed dog. Ceri has great enthusiasm for everything but Jack must have been standing at the back of the queue when they were distributing it. My friend Jack is shy, nervous, frightened and retiring and the difficulty with him is getting him to show any interest at all.

With Ceri I present myself as the man who provides exciting work. With Jack I must appear to be his best friend and demonstrate that there is no chance of my ever asking him to do anything at all that looks remotely like work.

Though we literally rescued Ceri from an owner who didn't understand him, Jack has more of the characteristics that I would expect that type of rescue dog to have. Each dog presented (and presents) a different set of problems but both need rescuing from the fears that beset them.

> *If there was a standard philosophy that applied to all dogs it would be that love, kindness and sensitivity will always win the day.*

If there was a rule it would be that there is no rule. If there was a common wisdom it would be to recognise that Ceri and Jack have different fears which stem from different causes and, therefore, each needs different treatment.

Jack: At Ease and More Confident

Well, I must say that more progress has been made than I could have realistically hoped for. In himself, Jack is at ease and more confident. Providing I do not put any kind of intense concentration on him he will do as I ask, usually almost immediately. A working Border collie moves with athletic speed and agility whereas Jack moves as though some time today will do. No, not that bad, I exaggerate; but his response is leisurely. And in that leisure lives a new and much-improved confidence. There is no twitching, no nervous expression, no concern that no matter what he does it will not be right.

> *Now, there is an expression of confidence in Jack's eyes and for me that is a huge reward.*

I would be oversimplifying if I said that our recent training sessions were the only factor responsible for turning Jack from a much-disturbed dog into the normal member of my canine pack that he has now become. Over and above everything we have achieved in the past few months, an earlier and very significant change in Jack's life influenced his recovery: the provision of a peaceful, outdoor kennel, a home that really suited him. Thus it would be true to say that two main ingredients, in equal measure, have been responsible for Jack's transformation.

I described earlier Jack's extreme dislike of the kitchen where he slept at our Shropshire home – the interminable noise of the washing machine, the vacuum cleaner and, worst of all, the unpredictable monster that turned itself on and off, the central heating pump.

With our subsequent move to Wales and his new, quiet, outdoor kennel and gravel yard his behaviour and demeanour underwent a dramatic change for the better. He could come and go as he pleased and was never 'shut in' and, you will recall, some of his particularly unsavoury habits were cured, specifically his penchant for eating other dogs' poo. His cosy bed of fragrant meadow hay made an impression on him just as he made a comfortable impression in it.

Finding a good place to be – his safe, cosy, outdoor kennel – probably contributed fifty per cent toward Jack's recovery.

What actually caused Jack to be so deeply disturbed, whether he was naturally of a very nervous nature or whether this was brought about by something that happened I shall never know.

I am content in his new-found ease and more than pleased that I found his 'magic button'.

There Is Always Hope

I hope my experience with Jack and Ceri shows that there is far more to the dog than is perhaps first apparent. It can be disturbed just as a human can and the causes for the disturbance can be many and varied.

A dog can be brought back from the unhappy place it occupies; it need not stay stuck in the bad place it finds itself.

Jack's 'magic button' was much less dramatic than Ceri's and much harder to find but, in the end, it worked.

Dogs live in their own world; it can be a happy or a disturbed place but they need not be locked away from us and our help. If we look hard enough and try to delve into what has made them disturbed we can find a way to improve things for them.

I will not just sit back, congratulate myself and simply end Jack's training, I will go on to try and make things even better for him.

Sometimes when I see photographs of a dog that I do not know I can see how content it is. It is just one moment in time caught in a single exposure of the camera's eye but it speaks volumes. The position of the body and the obvious joy I can see it has in doing what dogs do tells me all the good things I want to know.

Chapter Nineteen

To Sum Up – Did It Work?

I used two different approaches on two quite different dogs. The only thing each dog's training had in common was using gentle methods and my system of walking, turning and stopping. Both dogs graduated to word commands plus body-language signals, and responding to whistles was added to Ceri's repertoire.

I looked for a 'magic button' for each dog and found one of them surprisingly quickly and spent months looking for the other.

In the end I found both.

Did it work?
It most certainly did and it happened in well
under six months, quicker than I first thought
it would with both of my dogs.

My magic button concept will hopefully by now be understood.

What it means is that there is a motivator for every dog, we just have to look hard and find it. Once found the 'magic button' enables the dog to make very rapid progress because the training method it indicates will avoid the area of fear that is holding back progress. Training will, instead, be natural and liked. There will be an incentive – enjoyment – that provides a driving force, because the dog is not frightened by the training method.

What you are looking for is enthusiasm
rather than fearful compliance from
your dog.

Let me start with Ceri. He was a rescue dog in that he spent most of his first six months – that most impressionable period between being a puppy and a young dog – with an owner who failed to understand him. His attitude toward me, and I imagine to any other person, was that things were likely to get worse rather than better; that although I was being nice to him it could not possibly last – he expected inconsistency, believed it was normal.

At the beginning of his training anything that looked too

serious or had too much of my focused attention behind it was something to avoid at all costs.

He would not have been excited by training in obedience or agility and neither would have satisfied him because he had too much of a need to do the herding work he was born for. Both would have been pale imitations of the thing he was bred to do, that he was cut out for. Ceri needed to work in true sheepdog fashion.

A lot of dog trainers and behavioural therapists stubbornly resist the idea that there is no substitute for work and believe (quite incorrectly) that some sort of calming will take a working dog's mind off the very thing its breeding designed it for. Work calms!

The minute I started to train Ceri with ducks he came alive. The energy that would have previously gone into fear and suspicion of all things human was now centred on real, satisfying work.

He changed his appearance and attitude toward life virtually overnight.

Some breeds of dog are hardwired for a particular task. I know quite a lot of dog trainers and behavioural therapists who just cannot understand the mentality of the working breeds and they try to calm the excitement they see in these dogs without realising that it needs to be given full rein and set free. If it is suppressed it will, instead, become manifest in all sorts of behavioural difficulties which may become deep-seated.

Before I started the training with the really close observation and hard thinking that it entailed I had not realised just how different Ceri is from Jack; strange really, because they are half-brothers – same father, different mothers. But what is white to Ceri is very dark black to Jack.

Jack's training method took a lot of looking for and had to be very carefully thought out before any progress could be made.

I shall continue with the training of both dogs to try to satisfy them so that they are happy in their lives and with me.

I am super-sensitive about deciding on anything unless I am absolutely sure that the method is right. When I was growing up it was, on the whole, the parents – and in my case, my father – who decided what their children would do in terms of work. Never mind about what my talents were and what my natural skills might have been, the authority was his but his understanding of me was totally lacking. I dutifully did what he told me to do by settling for becoming a chef because, in his words, 'It was a way to earn money in a creative fashion', when all along I wanted to be an artist. Later I realised that the way to true happiness is to do what you really want to do and I became a (very happy) artist in a studio rather than a kitchen.

The poor dog does not have that same luxury of choice but is made to live as its owner decides, even if this is the opposite of what it desires and needs.

Fools Rush In . . .

My next point is a plea from both head and heart that you think hard about what you plan to do and only after a lot of careful thought set about training your dog.

Usually the dog will give you a clue about the right direction to take in so much as it will show less resistance to the things it wants to do and much more to the things it does not want to do.

My walking, turning and stopping method of training will work but you might need to tune it so that it ideally suits your dog. And the exercise can be done on or off the lead, it will depend on which your dog likes.

Your dog might be task orientated, like Ceri, or shy of anything that looks too much like serious intent, like Jack. It might be like Mad Miss Floss, who you will read about in a later chapter, and just need gentle and considerate rehoming with comforting routines that reassure.

Whichever way you eventually choose to train your dog, continue to look carefully at it and take note and respond to whatever you see.

The line of least resistance is always the best road to travel.

Doubtless I am preaching to the owners who are converted, or want to be – the others would be unlikely readers of this book – nevertheless I feel compelled to emphasise that there is nothing worse for a dog than a human who is in love with authority but an absolute stranger to careful thought.

There are of course certain things that you want your dog not to do, and other things that you would like it to do but, remember, the apparently obvious route to achieving both might well be the least effective.

If the very least I achieve is making you think about your dog's problems and the direction that you should take, that will be a start. There is no single rule book or universal, stage-by-stage dictate on training 'the dog'. For a start, every dog is different and, therefore, the same behavioural problem might have totally different causes in different dogs.

Your dog is a thinking individual with likes and dislikes, fears and feelings.

It is much more than just a recipient of your will, it has a propensity for love and faithfulness that most humans would be proud to share. You can turn your dog into an unwilling and frustrated slave to your will or make it your happy and fulfilled friend.

My method of training has always been a matter of finding a suit that fits rather than attempting to make one that fits all sizes.

My objective is to achieve an harmonious and happy relationship between you and your dog. I realise that searching for and working out the clues as to how best to live with and train your dog can be as difficult as following a treasure trail – but both have the potential for the greatest rewards.

Chapter Twenty

Ask Not . . .

'Any man's death diminishes me, because I am
involved in Mankind; and therefore never send
to know for whom the bell tolls; it tolls for thee.'

John Donne 1571?–1631

If you are young, John Donne's too realistic reflection on
the certainty of the unacceptable will be brushed like dust
under the nearest next event. Thoughts of 'the end' will be
instantly and neatly forgotten, or more accurately, pushed
aside. If you are young, its inevitability is probably not

something that will concern you greatly. It certainly did not worry me overmuch in my youth.

Life is a lot like school summer holidays. At the beginning of the holiday there are still weeks ahead, the days pass slowly and time and the future do not need to be worried about. But as the weeks slip by and you start counting the days, not weeks, until the start of term, going back to school looms into worrying reality.

I am seventy-one, and though I certainly do not walk around all day in extreme agitation about my inevitable death, I am conscious that it spies on me through the window of my subconscious more often than it used to, and however much I shout at it to go away or dismiss it with a joke, it persists in coming back.

Death is relevant to me mainly because of my dogs and my worries for their future. It is also important because dogs do not live as long as we do and that fact raises several issues. For example, if you, too, are as old as I am it might be more considerate to let one of the older dogs at the rescue centre take your fancy.

There are several reasons for me to say this, not least among them that young dogs do what young dogs are designed to do and like to run great distances at great speed – whereas you . . . ? Well, let's not go there in any detail.

An older human will make a much more suitable companion for an ageing dog.

From both person and dog view this is true. Both of you will walk a little bit slower than used to be the case and both will be rather more content with less distance. If you are an older human you might understand much better the problems the ageing dog might be experiencing. In fact, it is pretty safe to say that you will. I can vouch for that.

The reverse, of course, is also true. If you are young and vibrant you will want a more adventurous exercise session than an old dog will be looking for. And from the old dog's point of view, living with an energetic, noisy family could be worse than staying at the rescue centre – though that last point is debatable and would obviously, also, depend on the circumstances.

> *The young family will do better with*
> *a puppy or at least a young dog.*

On a practical level these things need to be taken into account.

Dear Old Friends

There are other more draining aspects to the fact that neither dog nor human can live for ever.

So far I have managed to resist several offers to rehome various dogs, not because I could not cope with them any more, or because I don't want them, but because of the mathematics of my situation. With just a little bit of luck (or with God's help) I might just outlive my last dog, as they and I are all advancing into old age.

A bookie would not offer very good odds on the likelihood

of an old man outliving a young dog. Whichever way you look at it, matching like for like is a sensible (and much more sensitive) route to take. Logic flies out of the window of course when a love-at-first-sight moment happens. If you can make sure that head overcomes heart it will likely be better in the long run.

Out of my fourteen dogs several are showing signs that tell me age is winning the battle.

Bob (touch everything around me made of wood) seems to have made a good recovery from his canine stroke and now walks in a straight line instead of wobbling and veering to the left. Dear little Fadey seems to be losing but I hope and continually pray that she will rally: her sight is going very rapidly and I have to make sure that I am near her as she worries if I am not. I speak to her every time she looks unsure and I notice that the sound gives her my location sufficiently for her to turn toward me.

Fadey has always been irritable with other dogs although some of the growls are more about ritual than intent and I suspect that some of the dogs she continually growls at are those who are actually closer to her – we, too, are always rudest to the people we love most. I have noticed that Polly is the recipient of more of Fadey's aggressive or fear growls than any of the other dogs yet she is the one that Fadey will lie down and sleep next to.

In the process of her struggle with illness she lost most of her sight but copes quite well, thanks to members of her pack who stand close to her and to me always being alongside her to make sure that she does not walk into things. I have observed that dogs as they get old often seem to start losing sight at the edge of the eye so seeing what is to the side of them becomes difficult. I always approach Fadey from the front, in a direct line, to try to avoid alarming her and I have noticed some of the other dogs in our pack doing the same thing.

There is an even greater need for real consideration with a dog that is suffering with advanced ageing problems which is why I suggest that older people, living in a quieter situation – without young children, for example – will generally provide a home that an old dog will find much easier to live in, especially if it has been rehomed.

I 'Hope for the Best'

My older brother has an oft-used, favourite question which is, 'Who on earth would want to live to ninety?' The answer of course is, 'Someone aged eighty-nine.'

It is human nature to want our dogs to live forever or, at least as long as we do. Life, unfortunately, is never that considerate and because our dogs do not live as long as us we come inevitably to that awful moment when a decision we really never want to have to take has to be taken.

I have misgivings about deciding too quickly and residual guilt about waiting too long. A no-win situation. The best (what an inappropriate word 'best' is) I hope for is that the sad event may happen naturally. I'm sure you will feel the same way.

We had a little black and white cocker spaniel called Mandy who died very suddenly under the table while we were having lunch. It was pretty awful but at least there was consolation in the fact that she had not suffered.

The great difficulty is that there is seldom a clear moment when the decision to end your much-loved dog's life is unarguably the right moment. I have seen dogs come back to a good state of health from what looked like their certain end.

Bob, my oldest dog, looked as though the end was close but careful nursing and lots of love have turned him back into a strong and energetic dog. Fadey lay still for almost a fortnight, so weak that she could not raise her head from the bed; it looked for all the world as if her light was slowly and surely being extinguished and that there was no chance of her ever coming back.

I put a soft cushion in the shade next to the main doors of the building the kennels are in so that she could sleep in comfort and still be with the other dogs. Each night I said a prayer for her before I left to go to my own bed and each morning I looked in dread in case her kennel yard was empty of life. Somehow she was always there waiting for me.

I came to realise how much I love her when it looked, for all the world, as if our time together was drawing to an end.

There have been times where waiting to see what will happen has been the right thing to do but I have also waited too long in the hope that bad might change to better. I would consider myself to be really good at training and living with dogs but quite unsuited to making a strong recommendation on handling the end. I really am quite useless in this regard.

Some people, to my mind, are far too quick to make that

last decision. They seem to treat the end of a life as something less final than it is, almost as though there were all sorts of other options open to the dog, and the ending of its life does not really take into account that this is the only life it has. Taking its life away is taking *everything* the dog has got.

As a vicar I spent a lot of time with people who had lost their loved one and can remember many who grieved as much over their dogs as they did over people. They felt that they had to make apologies over their grief for the dog because, 'it was only a dog'. The word 'only' is the villain here.

How can 'only' in any way describe the best friend you ever had?

How can 'grief' fit into the same sentence as 'only'?

I also cannot help noticing that of all the people whose funerals I have conducted none had been 'put down' but had died; one way or another their lives reached a natural conclusion. I must confess that I am deeply puzzled about this comparison as it makes no ethical or logical sense.

Are we seriously saying that humans are so superior a life form that the duration of their span must not be tampered with whereas the dog which comes under our domain can be terminated at a moment of our choosing?

I expect you, like me, will have mixed feelings on this issue.

I had a white duck, probably an Aylesbury, when I was five or six years old. It followed me around and liked to be made a fuss of. When the fox got it I was heartbroken and even now, a lifetime later, I can remember how very sad I was. What had been dear to me and very much alive was now just a few white feathers. To a little boy it did not seem just and now the man copes about as well as the child did.

If I look back and rationalise my behaviour as that little lad I find that nothing has changed. I do not find that age has added even one ounce of cynicism or robbed me of that tendency to always hope for the best. I do not find myself saying with what some would describe as wise hindsight, 'Ah well, it was only a duck.'

It was my duck and it loved me as I loved it. Love has nothing to do with the species of the recipient.

All Life Is Sacred

As a priest in the Anglican church the nature and direction of my religion must be obvious to all but I do find many of the Tibetan Buddhist views are closer to my own. Animals are regarded as sacred there. On television a man was shown tending the broken wing of a crane and feeding it until it had recovered; he was following the Buddhist belief that a good deed done on earth will bring its reward in their version of heaven. A markedly different philosophy to the Western habit of shooting anything that moves.

I find myself saying Amen to the Buddhist philosophy of refraining from taking life, and its emphasis on the value of living every moment of existence.

One day I shall have to defend the way I have lived which also means re-examining the way I thought. I can live comfortably with my belief that all life is sacred. I would borrow John Donne's idea and rewrite: The loss of any creature's life diminishes me because I am part of creation.

When a dog, or any pet or, for that matter, a person dies

one of the things that can hurt us most is guilt. The pain of guilt is almost equal to that of the bereavement itself. Often, we look back and wish that we had been kinder and much more sensitive. If we believe that we did none of those things as well as we ought to have done that will produce a pain inside us that may last until our own death. After the event you can't go back and put things right. It needs to be done now. On this very day!

I must admit that my mind has been much more peaceful when I have looked back and been able to say, 'I did everything I possibly could' and not find the need for 'except . . .'.

Chapter Twenty-one

Annie: Nervous Wreck to Shining Star

I found Annie on a busy road. She was my first Border collie though at that time I knew so little about the breed that I thought she was just a black and white dog. Once I knew that she was truly lost and that no previous owner would come out of the woodwork and claim her I set about training this extremely nervous rescue dog.

Annie came to me at the beginning of my career as a dog trainer and I did some things then that I would do differently now. If I were starting again I would begin by buying a book about the breed and its herding ability and, although this would not have changed my training method then it would have told me much more about the predispositions of the Border collie.

When I started training Annie, I don't remember having a specific objective beyond teaching her to respond and hopefully to eventually become more relaxed. I had no idea that one day she and I would work together herding sheep.

Her training was helped by my need for her and hers for me. Finding her had coincided with the collapse of my advertising agency business and a rapid descent into poverty. However, not having a job had given me a surplus of empty hours so her training was full time. I devoted myself to it.

Running away was Annie's answer to every unexpected noise or flapping thing.

I had quickly fallen head over heels for her and did not want to run the risk of her running away from me. To lose what I had found would have been a blow beyond the bearable.

She was nervous of unusual surprises but quite calm about others. A plastic bag flapping in a hedge would send her dashing away to – I don't know where. A lemonade bottle in the car fizzed suddenly and sent her leaping on to Maureen's lap for comfort – not a good idea as she was driving down a motorway at seventy miles per hour. The sight of a hot air balloon or the sound of a flushing toilet would shatter Annie's nerves completely and a brass band striking up would bring about a running-into-the-far-distance panic. But, strangely, a herd of escaped bullocks dashing round a corner of a country lane would delight rather than terrify her.

I knew nothing of dog whispering but realised that this most nervous of dogs needed very sensitive and gentle treatment.

Work Calms a Working Dog

Task training started the healing process. Practising learning to walk four paces to the left or right at any speed, or to run in a wide or a narrow arc, began to settle Annie's nerves and with her growing competence and her newly found confidence came a new calmness.

Memory always makes things seem simpler than they actually were and progress was, in fact, slow. It must have taken at least three years to make Annie begin to relax. She had been with us for about a year when we moved from our home in a village near London to rural Devon, where she was presented with the opportunity to start working sheep. She found this so absorbing, and tiring, and indeed satisfying, that after a year in Devon she was all but mended.

Bearing in mind her nervous state Annie achieved much, ultimately working expertly in demonstrations in front of thousands of people every single day at theme parks – a pretty amazing accomplishment for a dog that started as a nervous wreck.

If she was absorbed in a task that overtook her worries then the task itself became the only thing worth concentrating on and left no room for Annie's fears. I swear that she was so involved with the job of controlling the sheep during our theme park demonstrations that she did not notice the noisy ranks of people milling around the perimeter of the trials field. I certainly noticed no difference in her attitude whether working before the crowds at theme parks or on the quietest farm pasture. The task, her sheepdog compulsion to herd, was all that ever mattered to Annie.

There is an object lesson here for both nervous dogs and nervous people – if the task is totally absorbing it can quell the fears.

I remember a church gardener who had a stammer so severe that everyday conversations proved a huge trial. It hampered his life enormously. One day in church, in front of a large congregation, he read the Old Testament lesson. Knowing the passage was full of unpronounceable tribe names and places I found myself worrying for him as he walked up to read but I needn't have; he delivered a faultlessly smooth and powerful reading. Whenever he sung a Psalm with a complicated melody he would surprise everyone with his note-perfect, word-perfect rendering yet back in the churchyard he would revert to his disabling stammer.

I do not think that he was able to see what he had just done in any objective fashion. Had he been able to do so, I think he would have been able to move on unrestrained and unshackled to a much brighter (certainly more pleasant) future. The remedy he needed was with him all the time. If the task is all-absorbing it can overcome nervous difficulties. If you are going to train a nervous dog well this is a lesson not to be missed.

Skilful in Action

On farms there are often occasions when there is need to give medicine to every one of the sheep, and that can mean hundreds. If you are in a farming area and you see lots of sheep with patches of various colours daubed all over their wool it is, most likely, to tell the shepherd what treatments the sheep have received – a moving record that the shepherd can read as easily as you read this book.

Lower costs mean a better chance of seeing some profit and, because expensive equipment was beyond their budget, many of the small farms in North Devon practised what was known as 'dog and stick' farming which meant that greater reliance was put on the shepherd and his dog. The limited money available in the small farm's budget certainly would not buy sophisticated equipment such as a sheep race – a hurdle corridor that enables the shepherd to easily stream and direct sheep through it making all sorts of tasks much more manageable.

Our own sheep were gathered up in time-honoured fashion, into the corner of a field with only the dog providing a 'fence' to stop runaways. It was quite an experience, my favourite task in fact as it was a real test of the dog's and the shepherd's skills.

Certainly, when it came to drenching sheep, two more hands than the available issue would have been useful. Each sheep has to be caught, have its mouth opened then have a metered dose of drench administered followed by a spray marking to its back to tell the shepherd it has been treated.

I felt a bit like a circus juggler when I was surrounded by hundreds of woolly sheep packed into a small area, each one intent on escaping, marker spray tucked into my shirt, drenching gun in one hand, the other, somehow, free to catch a sheep. I would often drop the spray can or the 'crayon' during this demanding dexterity test and it would land under a forest of cloven, sheep-poo-encrusted feet all bustling and moving in different directions. Only Annie's great herding skill would give me the opportunity of picking it up again.

Several hundred milling sheep, each with a low centre of gravity and permanent 'four wheel drive', can overturn even the most sure-footed operator and it was only my very skilful dog who prevented me falling on to that less than spotless piece of pasture.

Annie was by far the best sheepdog I had so far seen because she seemed to understand the process as well, if not better than we humans did. The other dogs would need reminding constantly to 'keep 'em up' – at drenching time that call would echo around the Devon hills. But Annie was the only dog I have ever known that could patrol the outskirts of the flock to keep them tightly packed as well as directing the treated sheep away from the epicentre of that congested, woolly and pleasantly pungent chaos.

They are fond memories. Especially remembering the sun on my back and the ever beautiful Annie flowing fluently, unbidden, from one demanding task to the next. The greatest sight in all the world is an expert sheepdog effortlessly demonstrating its consummate skill. If the dog you are watching is your own and you trained it yourself, then the pleasure is even greater

In work mode Annie might have asked, 'Fear? What does that word mean?' Still, when she was not working and expected, instead, to socialise she was not quite at ease and small things would unsettle her.

Star Pupil, Picture Perfect

Perhaps the occasion that gave me greatest pride was the night I took her to the opening of an art exhibition at a posh London gallery. It was a real test of Annie's progress being so far from her normal experience in the quiet countryside.

The drive up from Devon was not too much of an ordeal and went fairly easily. When we arrived in London I tied a silver ribbon around her neck to show her at her best and then called a taxi for the last part of the journey. Getting her into a noisy taxi that stank of diesel was something of an ordeal, her anxiety made even worse by the busy traffic whipping by in both directions, but once in and tucked between my knees she found solace and made things bearable for herself.

When we arrived at the gallery the security man wouldn't let us in.

'No dogs in 'ere, guv. Rules is rules, more 'n my job's worth,' or something to that effect – I don't actually remember exactly what he said but my account fits his demeanour.

When I pointed through the window to the pictures of Annie hanging glamorously, perfectly lit, and explained that she was the model and I was the painter he weakened very slightly. After I had expounded and expanded to the doorman the personal risk he was taking in heartlessly – and with no thought for the commercial implication – denying artist and model access, as well as the outrage he could expect from my good friend the gallery owner, he reluctantly relented.

No pressure, then?

We were in! Annie, sanguine, dilettante, brushed until she gleamed and with her silver ribbon declaring her class, and me, quite well scrubbed up for a shepherd normally less elegantly attired – were ushered, together, into that hallowed space.

That evening Annie beat me paws down at eating sausages. A host of champagne-drinking socialites who looked as though they had just stepped off the catwalk fed her one gloriously tasty chipolata after another.

Annie, so different from the nervous waif I'd found on a busy road twenty-five miles from London, had passed what was for her the most demanding of acid tests. The training method I used with Annie set me up for all the dogs that followed.

Training the Nervous Dog: Fundamental Principles

- Be sensitive, be gentle and be both kind and very patient.
- Take one thing at a time, starting from the very simplest action such as 'lie down'.
- Don't spend more than five minutes on an exercise and never move on to the next until the one you are teaching has been perfected. (However, be prepared to be flexible: if your dog loves working then the full ten

minutes is just fine, even if the whole time is spent on only one instruction.)
- Be generous with praise and economical with anything that is not.

Out of the Darkness and into the Light

The only regret I have when I remember her is that she did not have any puppies – though she certainly helped to mother enough. When you do not know the dog's history chances cannot be taken. Though, now, I wish that I had!

Did the exhibition sell any pictures? I can't remember. It was hardly of the greatest importance to a shepherd with a job he loved and the best, and happiest, sheepdog for miles around. The artist had been overtaken by the shepherd and real life had begun.

Looking back at all that I have done in my life, training Annie and changing her from the most nervous creature into an extremely confident working sheepdog ranks higher than everything else, and I believe it always will.

When I remember the dirty, thin, worried little scrap of dog I found on the road and compare that image to the strong, clever sheepdog so very much at ease in her work and with her own world at her feet, I am both proud and happy. Her transformation was a great gift to her and an even greater one to me.

As I finish writing this chapter I look up. Just above the computer screen hangs a painting I did of Annie. She is standing in the shade of an apple tree, its rough bark contrasts with the juicy summer grass that hides her paws: a picture of contentment brought about by her newly found confidence.

The lesson that I take from all of this is that the benefit of good training is not just a well-behaved dog (though that would please most). Good training provides something far more meaningful for the dog because it experiences a kind of renaissance, it is rejuvenated. Training brings it happiness and ease of living as most valuable bonuses – benefits probably unforeseen by the owner at the outset of the exercise.

A Word of Thanks

Annie worked until she was thirteen years old. In the end she had to go to the vet for treatment but did not come back. Because I was working Maureen took her. When she returned without Annie the tears streaming down her face told the story of what had happened only too clearly.

I picked Annie up from the vet's surgery. She was still – lying on a cold tile floor. I can remember thinking that the least they could have done was wrap her in a blanket. This was my beloved.

When the grief stopped biting quite so hard I realised just how lucky she and I had been. We had worked together in the beautiful, rolling Devon hills for a long time. Both of us had been doing a job we loved and, most importantly, we were always together. When I remembered how sad she looked when I found her and how Devon became paradise for her, I thanked my maker for giving her to me.

Do you know, the only thing you can give away in great measure and still have more than you started with is love? Annie changed my life just as I helped to change hers.

Chapter Twenty-two

Monty (or Is It Alfie?)

Some stories make you cry, some make you smile and some can break your heart. Some stories make you wonder what kind of people can take a dog and, presumably, love it for a while and then simply pass it on like an old, unwanted, secondhand coat.

'Not my problem! It is only a dog.'

In the same world there are people who will change their lives in order to save the lost.

When I went to a silent retreat prior to being ordained as a priest in the Church of England I was mightily impressed by a lecture given by John, Bishop of Plymouth. All that he said found a willing roosting place in my mind, especially his prayer at the end of his talk. 'Lord we pray for the last, the least and the lost.'

Monty was certainly lost and most definitely treated as the least.

If you looked at him you might say, 'Ah, a Border collie.' Closer inspection would inform and encourage a different line of thought. Where did those long hairs on the eyebrows come from? Why is his muzzle square like a terrier's?

A good look at Monty invites you to consider a lot of different breeds but Border collie would certainly be one of them as his coat is the classic black and white – the right colours and in exactly the right place.

Monty was sent from Ireland to England because the chances of rehoming him were greater here – apparently Ireland has many homeless dogs. He then had four homes in England with rescue centres in between. And all of this had been packed into thirteen months of what must have been a very unhappy life.

Throughout this time he had been tracked by a lady called Valerie who had seen him on a website set up to help small rescue centres rehome their animals. Valerie liked the look of him, and no doubt felt sorry for this dog that nobody wanted.

Meanwhile, Monty's fourth home had turned out to be as much of a failure as the previous three and he'd been returned, yet again, to the rescue centre. It was to be his last chance. Aware of Valerie's interest, the lady who ran the centre called her and offered Monty to her. Valerie took up the offer and passed Monty over to her daughter, Jo, who she reasoned would give Monty a home where he'd have a real chance of finding happiness.

I feel like saying, 'Pheeew!' at this point.

'Alfie!' 'It's Monty, Actually'

Can you imagine what was going on in that poor dog's head? I don't think that humans would rate very highly in his estimation. If he never trusted them again it would not be surprising. Why should he put any faith in them or form a bond with them? What a lousy species they must be!

Now, all of a sudden he was in his fifth home and he's wondering, assuming, that the catalogue of his misfortune is set to continue.

What Monty did not know, and certainly would not have believed, was that things were going to get a whole lot better.

His new owner, Jo, was not like all the others. For a start, her job involved helping other people to deal with problem dogs so she knew an awful lot about dogs, especially those that had problems.

There is yet another twist that I can unravel right away for you, but took a long time to unravel for Monty. When he was first sent to England someone wrongly recorded his name as Alfie but this was only discovered when Jo looked through records that had come with him from Ireland.

I want you to imagine that people call out to you in the street but instead of using your name they use another. Would you react? No, of course you would ignore them completely.

So poor old Monty, the dog who never
obeyed or took any notice at all of humans,
was blamed for not listening when
they called him Alfie.

No doubt the people who called out the wrong name repeatedly thought that Alfie was either deaf or stupid. I can just hear them running him down.

What a shame it is that dogs can't talk human.

'Actually, my name is Monty.'

How simple that would have been.

He Bites, He Pulls, He Runs Away . . .

If I were a dog and was given a choice I would choose someone like Jo to live with. But rather than I praise Jo too highly I'll tell you how Monty responded when he came to live with her and from this you will be able to see for yourself what Jo is like.

Monty was not averse to biting anyone in sight, especially if they made any kind of noise or a sudden movement. He would snap and growl if touched, especially if the touch was accidental or happened while he was sleeping. He lunged at any dog he saw and would run off and not respond at all to Jo's frantic calls for him to return.

Monty pulled on the lead like a charging bull and became close to demented over everyday things like the scent of foxes or cats in the back garden. Visitors to the house caused him to panic blindly and, even when the introductions had been made and his fears smoothed, he would still run at them and then proceed to jump all over them.

> *Jo began to think that Monty had some kind of canine autism. However much she tried, however loving she was toward him, she just could not get close to him and it seemed that he just wanted to be on his own.*

She could not begin to get through to him. He was lost!

As you have probably gathered by now, Jo is quite remarkable. She has never actually said this to me but I can imagine her taking the line, 'What does not kill me makes me stronger.' I do know that she very often came close to giving up and that tears were usual rather than rare.

If you read again all of the things that disturbed Monty does and then ask yourself if you could deal with it, then there is probably only one possible answer.

On top of all of this Monty had his leg broken by a car and Jo – and Monty of course – lost Patsie, Jo's other dog to whom Monty had been very much attached.

I don't know about you but I feel I need a break after this harrowing story. I need time to think. Time to realise all that this dog has gone through and why he is as he is.

Time to appreciate that while some people abdicate all responsibility and throw a dog's life out the window others will devote their time, life and thought to giving it a home, not just any old home, but a very special one.

Keep an Open Mind

I took twenty minutes off during the writing of this story to walk my two house dogs, Ben and Misty, down a sunlit drive between avenues of beech trees. I counted my lucky stars and theirs. They have had a secure and loving upbringing, they are calm and happy, they respond instantly to even my *thought* call to come back.

Maybe I ought to have called this chapter Jo and Monty. I cannot describe in detail here the full extent of all the training and care that Jo and her husband Kaan have given to Monty.

I can say that they used non-violent methods and that they treated him as though he was undergoing recuperation from trauma (which he was) with great sensitivity and bucketsful of persistent love.

Jo joined an online forum where dog therapists and trainers exchange views. Members can ask questions on how to overcome difficulties with their problem dogs and get a great variety of useful answers from a host of knowledgeable dog behaviour consultants. They are open-minded people who realise that there is rather more than just a tired old mantra to solving the many difficulties faced when resettling a troubled dog.

(You might find this site as useful as Jo did: N4C (Network for Compassionate Canine Care and Communication) can be accessed from www.workwonders.org)

The professional dog world is populated by a wide variety of people. There are the theorists who have studied one method and decided that constitutes the whole world for them so will not look any further. There are those who know it all so why bother studying anything. There are those who follow the edicts of a dog trainer who has become a kind of holy prophet in their mind and chant systematic and so-called 'holistic' answers like a tired old tune without ever truly understanding the notes.

Then there are those who have realised that no one can grasp the whole range of unfathomable secrets that would tell us what is really happening in the dog's mind and they remain open-minded enough to look for better answers.

It is this last quality that I found so inspirational in the story of Jo and Monty. Jo just kept looking and kept on asking, and when things seemed to be getting worse she tried harder.

There is a wonderful section in the science fiction writer Robert A. Heinlein's *Stranger in a Strange Land* that deals with truth being coloured by assumption. Heinlein's story features a professor trained in observation and recall whose job it is to report without bias on events as well as providing a 'live record' or an absolutely truthful history. One of these witnesses is asked, 'What colour is the house on the hill?' Her answer is, 'It is white on this side.'

Behind the bad side of the dog that you can see could be another just waiting to get out. To assume that it is a totally bad dog because of what you have managed to see so far leaves no future for it, or you.

Jo's greatest virtue to my mind is the fact that she did not judge the whole on just a part but pushed on toward a much-improved future.

The people who are really interested in the welfare of their dog (and all other dogs) will read this book. Those that feel they know it all will not, which might go some way to indicating why there are so many badly behaved dogs out there, for nothing is worse than an owner with a closed mind.

Leave No Stone Unturned

Jo tried just about everything, even going to an animal intuitive counsellor. A friend told her about a lady who worked with animals using intuitive counselling and flower essences. Jo's version of this is that it helped her to see Monty in a more positive light and that it made her realise that he had so many problems that it would take a long time to work through them.

I strongly suspect that the session might have made Jo happier but done very little to help Monty but I ought to add that my faith in the ephemeral as opposed to the real and the practical barely exists. The real point though is not my scepticism but that she left no stone unturned in her search for anything that would make Monty's life better.

You will be delighted, I am sure, to hear that Monty is recovering. He still pulls on the lead, still lunges at other dogs and still has not become the perfectly behaved dog, but

Jo can now kiss him on his nose without fear of him biting hers.

She can stroke him all over without a single growl in return and, now, Monty wags his tail when he sees her, as Jo puts it, 'As though he loves me.' I would bet my bottom dollar that he most certainly does.

Jo and Monty still have much progress to make and Jo still struggles to achieve things that other owners would take for granted. Of one thing I am sure, even though their journey still has many miles to travel, Jo has enough patience and determination to go as far as it takes.

The truly rewarding thing about a rescue dog is that after trying for so long the moment is suddenly, and often totally unexpectedly, reached and the satisfaction realised from this new relationship is beyond price.

Chapter Twenty-three

Moses Meets His
Good Shepherd

I don't know if he was called Moses *by* his previous owner, or *by* his current owner *because* of his previous owner or because of what the dog did. I shall tell the story then you can decide which you think is the most likely.

It is an autumn morning in a rural Welsh valley. The farmhouses are strung out with something like a mile between each of them. It had been raining on and off for days, sometimes very heavily, and this combined with a high tide had pushed the river over its banks to make an inland sea in the trough of the valley. The mist clouds cut off the tops of the mountains and fill the valley with a sticky silence.

The sheep have gone walkabout to where they knew the grass was good. They had walked out of home field, turned right on to the road, passed through a country crossroad and walked a couple of miles to just one field away from the village. Here, there was an island between the tidal river and a wide drainage ditch, especially made for such flood situations as this one. In the middle of the island there is an abundance of good grass sufficiently lush to tempt peckish sheep.

No one saw them go but sheep leave evidence of the route they take: for owners whose dogs regard such evidence as a great delicacy my picture is clear enough.

Once on the island the flock had put their heads down and concentrated on the serious business of lunch. The river continued to rise until it was impossible to see where the paths were and before long most of the lower ground of the surrounding fields was shin-deep.

A local farmer, seeing the empty field and guessing where his sheep might have gone, sets out with his best sheepdog to bring them back. They track the signs easily, and successfully follow the trail for three miles or so until they reach the little village.

From the top of a hill the farmer can see his sheep. They are gathered on slightly higher ground between the water of the river and the drainage ditch which is now brim full so, in effect, his sheep are well and truly marooned on an island and the water is still rising.

They try for all they are worth to move the sheep through the water back on to the road but however much they push them the sheep are unwilling to enter the water, which for them is now belly-deep.

I can remember when I was a shepherd in Devon and a ewe and a lamb got stranded on a tiny island just how hard they are to move, even if they are manhandled – they know that the water is dangerous and cling to the safety of dry land. I remember, too, just how waterlogged sheep can get.

Natural Ability Will Out

An unknown dog appears suddenly on the brow of the hill. It is brown and black with a smooth coat, tall and leggy – obviously part Border collie mixed with—? At this distance, hard to say. The newcomer, obviously fascinated by the struggles between sheepdog and sheep, begins to move toward them.

I wonder what went through this dog's head when he saw something that must have rung bells for him? The urge, or compulsion, to work is knitted into the very fabric of the herding dog and here, right in front of it, was an opportunity that the dog just could not resist, a scene of great excitement with the urgent calls and whistles of the shepherd plus a hundred or so sheep.

The dog comes even closer. Then, without invitation, he joins in.

He was strong and full of energy and for a dog that had never been taught to work sheep showed an impressive natural ability. The farmer admired the way the newcomer worked and to the best of his ability helped both dogs by directing them with hand signals, whistles and shouts until, before long, the dogs were making progress, pushing the sheep slowly toward high ground.

Eventually the wet and muddy sheep were back on the road and the farmer's dog settled down to the task of taking them back; sheep that have been harassed like these had been will think only of going home, so no more resistance was expected.

As for the new dog, it stopped, unsure about leaving the village where it obviously lived. The farmer, guessing it must belong to someone close by, waved his arm toward the village and shouted at the dog to go back home – which seemed a poor reward for a dog that had helped him so much. The dog didn't want to go but after a while was persuaded to leave and in the end it vanished between the houses.

On his way home, the farmer pondered on what he had just seen, wishing that he had a dog like the leggy stranger. In terms of being directed, he could see that it was unfamiliar with driving sheep, but recognised its potential and wished that it was his.

Several days went by until, one morning, a neighbour came along in a tractor with a link box attached, and poking out of the link box was the head of the black and brown dog.

'It's not mine,' shouted the farmer. 'It belongs to someone in the—'

'He doesn't want him,' came the visitor's reply. 'You can have him if you want him.'

A Cross Made in Heaven

Moses belonged to the vicar who had got him when the dog was just weeks old. A cross between a New Zealand Huntaway and a Border collie the dog had proved too strong and energetic for the vicar to handle. On top of that, it would chase cars – a speciality of a bored sheepdog. Somewhere in the back of its mind it knows that it was born to work and cars make good, if exceedingly dangerous, substitutes for flocks of sheep.

Given the dog's history, any self-respecting shepherd would know its potential as a sheepdog. The Huntaway is a strong driving dog that can move huge flocks of sheep by means of loud barks and the strength of its determination; the Border collie is famed for moving sheep in a precise manner. So, there was Moses – or whatever he was called at that point.

The farmer was overjoyed with his gift and his unexpected good fortune, and over the years Moses earned a place in his new owner's 'best dog' category for his strength and reliability.

I can imagine the unrestrained joy Moses must have felt when he found himself living on a sheep farm with all of the freedom that kind of life brings. No more boring walks on a lead at snail's pace around the village but the freedom to run and to do what he was bred to do.

Luckily for the dog and his new owner a neighbouring sheep farmer had seen their struggle to rescue the sheep from the flood waters and had recognised the dog's talents. To the uninitiated, the dog's behaviour might have been misinterpreted as 'bad' rather than a desperately strong need for doggy fulfilment, a real cry for help. When the sheep farmer heard that the vicar would be relieved to part with his 'unruly' dog, he immediately suggested his fellow farmer – and the rest is history.

The Clues Are in the Picture

Though to a town dweller's eyes the countryside may seem empty of people there is always someone close by who either sees what is going on or can read from the evidence what has gone on.

I can remember many years ago going to paint a picture in a remote pine forest and because I had left my palette at home decided to use a piece of slate that I found in a ditch. There was definitely no one else there. I was alone.

When I finished I dropped the paint-daubed slate into a deep, overgrown drainage ditch and went home, picture under my arm.

Maybe as much as a month later I met the gamekeeper in the village shop.

'How did the picture of the pine trees turn out?' he asked.

I was absolutely amazed!

'How do you know I had painted a picture of pine trees? You didn't see me, I'm sure you were not around.'

He told me he had found the slate I had used in the ditch.

'But how did you know it was me?' I was puzzled.

'You're the only one who paints around here,' he said.

'Ah, but how did you know I was painting a picture of the pine trees?'

'The colours on the slate gave me all the clues I needed.'

The moral to that little tale is that other people see what we do more often than we think.

It might be a good idea, before seeking professional help to ask someone you see often

and who has a well-behaved dog what they think
you might be doing wrong with yours.

If their (unbiased) advice is as perceptive as the game-keeper's observations it might just be worth a try.

Breeds Fit for Purpose

Moses has long gone to that place in the sky reserved for dogs but the evidence of his time on the farm can be seen to this day. Some of the young dogs have smooth coats flecked with brown and black and they are all too leggy to be pure Border collies.

I could just leave this story now but I want to extract some wisdom from it.

If a dog is the outcome of years of breeding designed to fit it for a task, its tendencies can't be cancelled out at the whim of its owner. The predisposition (or should I say irresistible compulsion?) will always be there. The dog, somehow, knows what its purpose is and that cannot be erased or changed – it will always be there.

The fact that an owner does not even recognise what the dog is telling him will serve to increase the frustration. A vicar, for example, leads a very different life from that of a sheep farmer and having done both jobs I can appreciate how frustrated poor old Moses must have been.

Vicars spend most of their time meeting people over cups of tea – 'More tea, vicar?' gives a clue about the extent of this activity. Maybe, at the end of the day – after writing Sunday's sermon or putting the final touches to the eulogy for tomorrow's funeral – there might just be a little time for a very restrained, fairly genteel, domestic stroll around a friendly farmer's field.

Sheepdogs don't stroll! Sheepdogs don't like leads. Bored sheepdogs chase cars.

The sheep farmer is on the move from first light to last, there are always sheep in the wrong place and there are jobs to do, all the time, that need the dog and the farmer to work as a team. The result is that the dog is always with the farmer. It is the sheepdog's natural place. That is where it likes and needs to be.

If you go for a herding dog make a note that it has to be fulfilled every day of its life. All the cuddles in the world will not soothe the passion and the need it has to work. Its brain needs to be exercised as much as its body does.

Small wonder then that poor old Moses was dying of frustration.

Taking a dog that does not suit your lifestyle is a mistake. Any dog is shackled to the lifestyle of its owner for a long period of time. It is all-important to make a sound judgement about the suitability of the match you are planning. If you get it wrong the frustrations of both dog and human will come home to roost with bad results. And it will be worse for your dog because you can rationalise your mistake while your poor dog is the victim of the slavery you have imposed on it. Strong words? Yes, I suppose they are, but putting the wrong dog in the wrong situation is like harnessing a racehorse to a milk cart.

If you want to find a way to bring about mental illness and behavioural problems this is a very effective way to achieve it.

Times Change, Dogs Don't

The trouble is that the world is moving on so fast that humans have difficulty in keeping abreast of what's happening in it, let alone what's going on with dogs.

Not so very long ago a whole host of breeds were designed by man for a purpose, among these are the hound group, gun dogs, terriers, running dogs and fighting breeds. Because their purpose has vanished many breeds of dog have had their real work removed and replaced with appearing at shows, or doing obedience or agility trials, or flyball or, and worst of all, going out for the twice daily, restrained walk on a lead around a block of houses.

If I could ask a Border collie if agility ranks alongside herding in terms of satisfaction I think I know what the answer would be and the same unfavourable comparison would be made by all of the other groups or breeds I have just mentioned. But agility or hard exercise are the best substitutes available.

If a breed has been developed over thousands of years to be fit for a particular purpose and then the purpose is removed, it is small wonder that so many behavioural problems exist.

To learn about dogs requires more than just owning one: you also need to take the time and trouble to realise what your dog is telling you and to notice, at the beginning, what clues you are being given by its physique and the breed it belongs to. A wise owner thinks very carefully about the suitability of dog to human and, more importantly, vice versa.

Moses, in a way, rescued himself but only because the farmer could see him in a discerning light. With the average rescue dog the task could be more difficult. It might not be possible to say what breed it is. It will be possible, though, to look at it objectively and ask, 'Does what I can see in this dog match what I can see in myself?'

It's athletic; am I? Is it calm or restless? Which of these sums me up? Is it young and energetic? Am I the same?

If Moses had not gone over the brow of the hill his life would have probably ended under the wheels of one of those cars he had been chasing through the village.

If you have a dog that is really misbehaving my advice would be to look closely at how you are treating it. Very few dogs misbehave without due cause. As I have said earlier, you need to try to put yourself in its place and understand the reasons why. There will be one.

Chapter Twenty-four

The Dog with No Name

The rescuer in this true story is called Imogen. She is married to Richard, but rather than describe them I have borrowed some of Imogen's words from the website she runs called Work Wonders with Your Dog at www.workwonders. org – the same site that Jo contacted N4C through when she was looking for help for Monty.

> For over 25 years I have worked with people and their problems and I am an Accredited Member of The British Association for Counselling & Psychotherapy.
> It might appear that working with dogs is a huge departure, but I have always lived with dogs, horses

and other animals, and I know first hand how important, challenging, rewarding and harrowing these
relationships can be.

I am especially aware of how problems with dogs
can impact upon other areas, and vice versa, and how
the loss of a much-loved pet can be devastating to us.

I started to train and find out more about dogs
while bringing up two pups and accommodating our
adult rescued terrier. They presented challenges which
were being exacerbated by obedience classes as I did
not understand the role of stress in a dog's life. I have
also become aware of the power of correct feeding for
the dog, and physical tensions and injuries and the
influence these can have on temperament and
behaviour. My dogs have also taught me a great deal
about how dogs talk to each other.

I offer my experience and continuing study and
interest in ways to get the best out of our dogs, answer
their needs, and engender cooperation, NOT force
compliance. I also welcome anyone finding difficulty
after losing a much-loved pet.

I recognise that my working life has been focused
upon helping people find their most comfortable and
rewarding place in their world. Now I am pleased to
say I can help to do that for dogs and their humans too.

When you enter the county of Cornwall a sign saying 'Yer
Tiz' ('Here it is') greets you. Sometimes when you are
travelling by car you will see a sign saying something like
'Last Garage in England'. In other words, you will not have
another chance to buy fuel for a long distance. Such signs are

a standard promotional inducement intended to work on our fears. Penzance, on the other hand, if it wanted to have a similar sign could legitimately – in as much as it's on the coast – say 'Last Land before Europe'.

In the ancient Cornish language Penzance was *Pen Sans* which means holy headland. Devon and Cornwall are full of holy sites because when the Irish brought Christianity to England their small coracles (described in ancient writings as 'leaves') landed mostly in the West Country. Newlyn, just up the coast, was the home to the Newlyn School of Painters, full of the same light and atmosphere that ever bathes this romantic place.

Here is a land of mist and moors, of sea frets, craggy cliffs, cream teas, lobster pots and quaint Bed & Breakfast signs.

Let me start at the beginning of my story.

Imogen and Richard, the heroine and hero of this adventure, live in an old farmhouse on the edge of a small village some sixty miles from Penzance. They have donkeys and horses and an old dog called Abou. If they look out of their window they can see open farmland and woods – a perfect place to calm and settle humans, and maybe a rescue dog.

A little dog somewhere between a wheaten-haired terrier and a poodle had been surviving by pilfering the contents of dustbins and no doubt scrounging tasty scraps from the thousands of tourists who descend on Penzance every summer. A dog with no name or history. A Penzance street dog. Seen for a moment out of the corner of the eye, then gone. How long she had survived in this situation is not known either.

In fact, there is more 'not known' about this dog than any I have ever heard about. Usually there is at least some sort of clue, like where a dog came from and how many owners it had known, but in her case, sorry, this is all I can tell you.

Eventually the little dog was picked up by the dog warden and put into municipal kennels. I expect they waited for someone to come and claim her. It would have been a long wait for no one apparently owned her – none cared, and none came forward.

Bonding

Imogen heard about the little dog from a friend who had seen her advertised in a local newspaper as a bearded collie cross, and after some careful thought set out to drive the sixty miles to Penzance with rescue in mind. It was pouring with rain, not the gentle kind but stair rods.

If ever you go to Devon or Cornwall you will notice how beautifully green it is. The reason is rain. It rains a lot! There is a joke in Devon that centres on the island of Lundy which is set some twelve miles from the mainland and occupied mainly by sheep and puffins: 'If you can't see Lundy it is raining. If you can, it is about to start.'

When Imogen arrived at the dog warden's kennels she was greeted by a sad sight, the kennel was outside and the little dog, well used to roughing it, was standing out in the pouring rain, soaked to the skin.

I would imagine that the sight of the little drenched dog with fur slicked to its body banished any remaining doubts Imogen might have had and before long both were in the car heading home. She had done it. For good or bad Richard and Imogen were committed.

'She barked all the way and didn't stop for a breath until the car arrived at the cottage,' Imogen recalls. 'And even then it didn't completely stop until she had been introduced to Richard.'

From this moment the dog had found her soul mate. As far as the little dog was concerned Richard was the human she had been looking for. He passed the test. He was not just all right – he was perfect.

> *She had fallen in love with him –*
> *he was her 'magic button'.*

They named her Floss and later added the words Mad Miss to describe her nature. Though she had no history the one thing they did know was that she bit everyone in sight which is not surprising given the unsettled life she had lived. Whether it was good fortune or destiny Floss had ended up in the best possible place. She now had a name, a home and something she had probably not known before: love. As a bonus there were eight acres of land to run in plus horses, donkeys and Abou to make friends with.

The donkeys believing that the little woolly Miss Floss was a sheep decided very early on that she needed chasing rather than making friends with so no luck there but Floss quickly settled in with her new family.

Training for Contentment

On the very first walk across open fields Richard persuaded Imogen to let her off the lead. She was reluctant and believed the little dog would make a break for freedom. When the lead came off she stayed by Richard's side and has chosen this as the very best place to be ever since.

Sometimes a bond is instantly made. I do not know what it is that makes this happen but it does. Floss had picked Richard and that is the way it has stayed.

The dog is a creature that will thrive on settled methods and routines. If you are driving somewhere and keep changing direction you will get lost and being lost adds both tension and stress in good measure.

I know Imogen because I am a member of her N4C forum and read her answers to the difficult doggy questions that are asked by the members and would describe her as stable, consistent and the possessor of a large ration of that rare commodity – common sense. She and Richard settled on the wisest of courses in as much as they tried to look at the possible end of the process while they were still at its beginning. They resolved their objective early. Training Floss was going to be much more about bringing contentment than it was about formal training.

I must confess to liking their objective a lot. This is an eminently practical way to settle a rescue dog: to give much but to expect little will bring about far more progress than planning to achieve a great deal.

The couple established routines for Floss that were designed to settle and calm her.

A dog that lives with routine quickly resettles because routine allows them to know what is going to happen next.

Because Floss had epileptic fits and seizures they changed her diet to one that was more beneficial.

Please Don't Pat the Dog

They also did something fairly unusual: they realised that people just sail in and pat dogs that look sweet whether the dog in question likes it or not.

I am always amazed when I hear of people who do not have the courage to tell the insistent patters of strange dogs that the dog does not like it. The outcome is nearly always that the dog eventually nips the intrusive person and then the bitten human makes a huge fuss that can turn out to be more devastating in terms of the end result than anyone expected.

I meet a lot of dog owners through my clinic page who never seem able to tell other people not to pat their dog and some of them allow the biting routine to happen several times rather than be firm with a total stranger.

Another dog behaviour associate of mine puts a fluorescent yellow bib on her dog when she takes it out for a walk and comments that strangers tend to ask why the dog is wearing it before they attempt to pat the dog. A very sensible thing to do.

If you never tell strangers not to pat your dog the dog will quickly realise that you cannot be relied upon and will become even more prone to defending itself. Floss calmed down reasonably quickly because she knew that her humans *would* look after her. The likely response from a dog – it will bite – to uninvited attention is likely to happen and the fact that the 'patters' of strange dogs cannot see the risk is beyond my understanding. But that is how it is and best that you are fully aware of it.

Calm People, Calm Dog

Floss is now well and truly settled with Imogen and Richard and though still an arch-enemy of the dog-chasing donkeys she has learned to deal with them. She is terrified of thunder and lightning storms, which for her lead to epileptic seizures, so she sleeps in a dog bed on Richard's side of the bed. If she is frightened she paws Richard who takes her down to his study and sits with her which gives Floss great comfort.

Apart from the routines and the thoughtful and loving care given to Miss Floss there is the fact that Floss has a rock to cling to. As yet, I have not met Richard but when I do I expect he will be calm, quiet and even-tempered. Mood is contagious – nervous, jumpy owners have nervous, jumpy dogs. Calm people mean calm dogs!

Make a Difference

There is a story I used to tell in church. I first read it myself in Jack Canfield's book *Chicken Soup for the Soul*. It is about a man who goes jogging on his favourite, deserted, beach every morning. One day he sees a figure in the distance that appears to be bending down and picking something up and then throwing whatever it is into the sea.

The jogger is curious about what the distant figure is doing so he jogs toward him. When he gets closer he can see what is happening. The stranger is picking up starfish stranded by the tide and, one after another, ceaselessly, he picks them up and throws them into the sea.

The jogger asks the man why he is doing this. The man answers, 'I am saving them!'

The jogger points out that this is a futile task as starfish have been stranded on every beach all the way along the coast. He ends with a question, 'What difference will it make?'

The stranger does not answer for a little while but then, as he throws yet another starfish back into the sea, he answers the jogger's question with a most meaningful comment:

'It made a heck of a difference to this one!'

Four years on from the rescue of Miss Floss Imogen tells me, 'She is a very loving dog, she loves to play, eat and sleep. She has an inner clock that tells her, and us, when it is dinner, breakfast time, and so on. She is relaxed as long as she is at home with us and her routines of feeding, walking and sleeping are adhered to.

'We do not think that she will make old bones but she is one of the most joyous dogs you could ever see running through a meadow!'

As the stranger on the beach said, 'It made a heck of a difference to this one!'

Chapter Twenty-five

Toby: I Don't Want to Be Alone

I want you to imagine that you are a small child – I would say puppy but that is too great a leap for the imagination to make. You do not remember much about your mother as you were probably taken away from her before you were ready or able to cope but in contrast to what is to come, they were happy times, albeit dimly remembered.

When you grew past the pretty baby stage you were thrown out on to the street. That may have been an instant event or a gradual process of neglect, but it happened. Here, there was no shelter; if it rained you got wet and stayed that way. If it was cold you simply got cold. You were thirsty but there was nothing to drink. The nights were long, uncomfortable and deeply unsettled.

When you wandered on to a road, cars nearly ran you down and drivers shouted at you. People out walking with their dogs waved their arms and shouted to drive you away. Who wants a stray intruding into their cosy world?

It never occurred to them that you had nowhere to go. In short, no one cared a fig about you.

There was no food, except perhaps stuff that could be scavenged. Because you were young and not physically strong or streetwise, you were a natural victim for anything bigger and stronger than you.

This is not a natural world where a dog can eventually learn to be at ease with its situation but a hostile, noisy and uncomfortable place where life itself is under constant threat. It is a dump where the unwanted are thrown.

The world, as you see it, is pretty awful and the worst creature in it is one that walks upright on two legs.

How would you cope with a life like that? What would it do to your trust or your sense of 'normal'? How would it affect your behaviour?

Eventually you are captured and locked in a cage. Suddenly there is food and water but there is nothing to do except sit there and wait. You can hear voices but no one comes to see you very often because they are too busy. Your whole life is controlled by others, you have become some sort of duty for the people who feed and house you, a number on a record of lost dogs.

After a while you are moved again, to another cage, and there you stay – until one wonderful day when some people come to see you. They really like you and after lots of fuss they take you home to live with them. You remember dimly that there were others who seemed to care, for a while. Life has suddenly got a whole lot better than it was.

The people in the house you have come to live in have routines, they come and go. They take you out for walks, they play with you and, though all of this is good, you do not understand it because it is new to you and foreign.

Perhaps you're wondering how long it will last?

I hope I have given you just a glimpse of what life must be like for the unwanted dog and that you have tried to really imagine how it must feel.

The Trouble with Toby . . .

This is the true story of Toby who was found by the police when he was about six months old. He looks just fine on the outside, glossy, medium size, a bit like a collie and a bit like several other breeds of dog. Inside, and unseen by most, there are still the scars of memories that will not be simply rubbed out.

Toby's new owners are called Andrew and Lorraine. Lorraine works in London five days a week but Andrew works from home, so Toby gets lots of company.

When they went to the rescue centre Andrew fell instantly in love with Toby, whereas for Lorraine the love took a while to develop.

The couple really have bent over backwards to give Toby the very best home. He is walked often in the parks and open countryside near their home and is certainly fed well. He has a comfortable bed in a warm kitchen and can look out through large patio doors on to the garden. All should be well.

Toby has a horror of being left alone: if it is in a car he is fine, but if he is left in the house Toby will try to eat his way out. He has never completely succeeded but he has made several jolly good attempts resulting in severely chewed doorframes and some fractured furniture.

Among their many efforts to discover why Toby does what he does, on a couple of occasions Andrew and Lorraine consulted dog psychologists, who generally concluded that Toby was being overindulged and given far too much attention. This, they told the couple, had resulted in him believing that he was the boss. The answer: he should be ignored and not pandered to. But I believe the treatment recommended for Toby was based on a superficial assessment of his behaviour rather than its underlying cause.

Misdiagnosis: Overlord or Underdog?

The fears that beset a rescue dog need to be lived with and observed over a long period of time. No fleeting visit or one-off observation will ever get inside a dog's head and unravel the troubles that have infected it.

Too often the 'pack boss' diagnosis is no more than a convenient red herring, a dangerous distraction from solving the great conundrum of what is actually wrong with the dog. It is a bit like asking someone for directions and having them answer that, as they don't know the way to the place you want to go to they will give you directions to another place instead.

A dog only becomes the boss if it possesses a huge share of self-confidence and that would hardly be found in abundance in a dog such as Toby, or any other that has had a deeply troubled and difficult past. An alpha dog knows only victory; defeat is an anathema. The rescue dog on the other hand has known nothing but defeat. So, how can continual defeat equip a dog to be boss?

Let me make a clear contrast for you. The pack boss of my tribe sits comfortably confident when he is left alone and does not try to dig his way to freedom because a more satisfying freedom exists where he already is.

> *Confident 'boss' dogs don't need to escape*
> *from their satisfying environment but*
> *frightened dogs do.*

Whoever wanted to escape contentment?

Toby's problem is much more likely to be rooted in his fear of being abandoned again. He will remember what that feels like and does not want a second helping. The one thing you don't do to the unsure is ignore them.

I have some rescue dogs and the very last thing I would ever do is pay no attention to them, neither would I be silly enough to imagine that I can leap the chasm between two species and claim to be able to rapidly put my finger on the dog's problem. Not unless I were some kind of fluent dog-speaking magician with great psychic gifts. I always take my time and base what I recommend on the careful observations that I have made: being thorough and painstakingly observant is more likely to uncover a truth.

For the rescue dog, the greatest medicine during this watching and waiting period is love and bags of attention. Would you respond to someone who constantly ignores you and shows no sign of love? I think the answer might well be NO. On a practical level, should you decide to 'cure' your dog by ignoring it, you may be replacing doorframes for a very long time.

I can remember when I painted pictures for a living how many amateur painters heralded a new type of brush or a new technique as the great improver of their skills whereas the truth was that their competence with all the brushes and all the techniques was the key to their problem. There is the wisdom, too, of the famous golfer, Gary Player, who when told that he was lucky responded, 'The more I practise, the luckier I get.' The same is true of dog training and the careful observation that leads to putting a problem right.

Dig Down to the Root of the Problem

Andrew and Lorraine have opted for not ever leaving Toby alone. Fortunately, as I have said, Andrew works mainly from home and at weekends, when he regularly covers football matches, Lorraine can be with Toby. On the rare occasions when neither of them can be with him, Toby is taken to a dog-walker or sitter.

Any cure for Toby's problems has to accurately address his fear.

Let's start by looking at the facts. What is the difference between being left in a car and in a house? One situation troubles Toby and the other does not. What is frightening about a house and what is it that makes a car acceptable to him?

A car is smaller and does not allow a lot of space for the pacing and puffing that often precedes and increases anxiety in a dog. It has all-round vision and is quiet. It is also more like being outdoors, in so much as there is a 360-degree view of whatever is going on outside the windows. For example, passers-by can be clearly seen as well as heard.

A house is totally different. There are solid walls and restricted opportunities to look out if you are as small as a dog. When someone knocks on the door, the dog hears the sound but the caller's identity and intent remain unknown, and what is not known is worried about.

And in a house there are – all the time – all sorts of noises to contend with: everything from fridges and boilers to plumbing, electrics and creaks in the fabric of the building itself, including some with a disturbingly high frequency which, as I've said before, offends the sensitive and acute hearing of a dog.

On top of this, the dog has doubts about whether all the members of the household have really gone out. Might there still be someone upstairs? The noises and any voices from next door can be heard much more clearly by your dog than they can by you. If there is a 'next door' on either side, the problem doubles.

Imagine that all sorts of unidentifiable sounds are coming at you from all sides, plus above and below, and that your hearing is hundreds of times better than that of a human.

Try to imagine the type of frustration that would come from listening carefully for the return of your people and having the sound you want to hear muffled and confused by all those other frightening noises.

And all this is before we even start to think about the dog's other highly developed senses.

So, the house can be a more worrying place for a dog than you might think. The obvious answer might be to make more use of the car if, like Toby, the dog seems happy there. But the English weather with its rapid switch from cool to hot would make it a totally unsuitable and unsafe place for any period longer than a very short one.

Consider the Options

I think that at this point I would examine two options for a dog like Toby: one is straightforward and the other more lateral-thinking.

First, can I duplicate the advantages of the inside of a car somewhere where there is no risk of it becoming like an oven? Secondly, would being left alone after a long and satisfying walk decrease the dog's anxiety?

With regard to option one, I might think about a kennel and run in the back garden. Of course, an urban situation is not like a country environment – it is noisier and dog owners need to show consideration for their neighbours. The dog would need to be acclimatised to it by gradually increasing the length of time spent in it. I might just add a few hollow toys that can be filled with peanut butter or some other sort of time- and interest-consuming filling.

I might reason that though he will still hear noise, Toby is an urban dog and quite used to the sounds and smells of his surroundings. I would also try option two, the long and tiring walk, before leaving him in either house or kennel, and then take my leave theatrically but wait, quietly, just outside and close enough to see what the dog is doing. Over several repetitions of both these ploys I would gradually increase the time the dog is left alone and observe whether the period without anxiety gets longer or not.

Given the time such measures would take to employ coupled with the busy nature of Andrew and Lorraine's work, I might end up doing exactly what they are doing and ensure that Toby always has company, but it would be nice to have an alternative for those occasions when finding someone to be with him proves difficult.

With a seriously damaged rescue dog the problems can often be part of the package in that they can be very deep-seated. The approach needs to be thoughtful.

In our family, when something goes awry, we have a standard joke based on Arthur Conan Doyle's Sherlock Holmes murder mysteries. 'Who dunnit?' we ask – Holmes might have deduced it was a left-handed, retired sailor who walked with a stick and used an Algerian snuff. Sorting out the troubled rescue dog's problems is a lot like detective work and it is observation of facts, not hunches, that leads to the cure. I always allow myself time to draw up a list of relevant options to deal with the problem and then try the most likely: often there is no need to look further but sometimes it remains a work in progress.

Toby Comes First

Apart from Toby's fear of being alone problem, and despite all his mental scars, Andrew and Lorraine have a very happy dog – all thanks to their willingness to change the pattern of their lives to accommodate him. They also try to focus on the many things he does well and reinforce his *good* behaviour.

Some might consider that the couple have been willing to change too much, many would not be prepared to go so far. Not surprisingly, I would disagree with them. We take on rescue dogs because we love them, not just at the start of the relationship but all the way through.

The difference between the erratic and consistent dog lover is what put the rescue dog on the street to start with and the rock-solid, long-term caring that took it and kept it off.

One is admirable, the other beyond any sort of merit at all.

When I think of the joy my own dogs give me then set this against the work they present me with, the positive wins every time. Coming home to a house without a dog is a fairly hollow experience, whereas being greeted by the wagging tail, the juicy, black nose and the kind of unreserved love that only a dog can give is an experience I for one am not prepared to live without.

I spent a pleasant weekend with Andrew, Lorraine and Toby. We walked over field and dale, through woods and down country lanes and both humans and dog enjoyed every single minute of it. When Toby and I played ball in the back garden I could see by his sparkling eyes and untiring devotion to the repetitive game what a truly happy chap he is. I am sure that, now and again, Toby remembers how his life used to be: the contrast must be beyond amazing. Thank goodness there are people out there who will go to any lengths to give a dog a home!

Chapter Twenty-six

Prince and a Donkey Called Tessa

I was in my early twenties, married with four small children, and lived in a village on the salt marshes of the River Crouch in Essex. Each day I caught a commuter train up to London to work in the advertising industry leaving Maureen to manage our small menagerie as well as looking after the children.

Although Maureen has always been marvellous with all sorts of animals my thinking showed little consideration. We had a yellow Labrador, a donkey and, for a while, something originally billed as a Newfoundland.

Essex is flat and windy but has (or at least had) some very good countryside walks. Some, along the banks of the tidal river, would provide more walking than even the most energetic dog and human would find comfortable. In winter a husky team and sled would be more appropriate as the cold winds from Siberia or Scandinavia would find little to hamper or limit them and the salt marshes would be deep in snow and battered by the coldest of cold winds.

We lived in a bungalow with a garden like an airstrip, long and narrow, and at the bottom, in a stable, Tessa the donkey lived.

One day, during a photo-shoot halfway up the country on which I was art director, I had passed a field and noticed that it was full of donkeys. When I spoke to a local I was told that they were going to that place that donkeys do not want to contemplate. In typically irresponsible and impulsive fashion I figured that I could afford to save one of them so, there and then, with no thought for the future, I paid my money and transported Tessa in a hired horse box back to Essex.

The journey took a long time and by the time we arrived the full moon was high in the sky. Tessa allowed herself to be unloaded quietly and bearing in mind that most of our neighbours would be tucked up in bed I was grateful for small mercies.

The difficult part was still to come. Tessa had to be walked up a long, straight, concrete path. The minute we stood on the hard surface I realised (partly) how difficult this journey was going to be. How on earth do you stop a donkey from clip-clopping? How, on a cold, clear, still and silent night do you minimise that penetrating and echoing clip-clop? The path ran past our bedroom, so it would be better for my health – bearing in mind I had not told my wife that I would not be coming home alone – if we could pass by quietly.

So far so good. We had travelled almost to the point of turning past the front door when Tessa demonstrated another donkey skill. The most enormous, wake-the-neighbours, raucous Heeeeeeee Haaaaaaw. Then another, but dropping the haitches this time, Eeeeeeeeee Awwwww.

It echoed around the village like the horn of a ship lost in fog! The worst thing in the world given the delicacy of the situation. The thing I least wanted to happen happened –the lights in our house went on. I froze as a rabbit freezes in the headlights. Maureen must have moved like lightning to arrive at the front door so quickly or perhaps me being rooted to the spot like Lot's wife gave her time. She looked in horror. The look and the silence seemed to last a long time.

A man, a donkey, a saddle and a bridle, all lit dramatically by the moon, standing outside her front door in the middle of the night. Not much room to manoeuvre. No likely stories sprung to my lips.

'What have you done now?' Not so much a question, really, but more a precursor to Maureen's forthcoming statement.

I made all sorts of noises told her how pleased the children would be, retold Tessa's sad story, but then it came:

'It's the donkey or me,' she announced.

The door was slammed shut. Tessa and I slept in the stable.

In the morning there was a dramatic recovery. Tessa greeted the day with her usual call. The children heard and came dashing down the garden, and Maureen came too. The love affair had begun. A beyond-resistance, love-at-first-sight relationship had been kindled. It lasted a long, long time.

This part of the story is happy and I should have quit while I was ahead but I didn't.

When Is a Newfoundland Not a Newfoundland? When It's Prince!

Not very long after I acquired Tessa, I brought home a dog from a rescue centre. He was black all over and huge. A great bear of a dog. According to the centre he was a Newfoundland. When I look at pictures of this breed I can see that he certainly was not one. He was similar, and maybe had just a touch of Newfoundland somewhere in his background but that was the closest he came.

He did not have the webbed feet of the breed who are famous for their swimming ability and he couldn't swim a stroke.

According to Wikipedia:

The Newfoundland dog excels at water rescue, due partly to their webbed feet and amazing swimming abilities. Newfoundland dogs require grooming at least once every two weeks. Extremely loving and patient, as puppies Newfoundlands are laid-back and considered easy to housebreak.

Doubtless a pure Newfoundland does have 'amazing swimming abilities' but Prince did not. I had rescued him from the fast-flowing waters of the River Crouch twice, both occasions being in the dead of winter and in a lazy wind – for those who don't recognise that countryman's description it means the wind, too lazy to go around you, goes through you instead.

I had to make a choice between getting into the water quickly before the tide carried him away or taking my clothes off first. Neither of these two choices could in any way be described as pleasant. Once in the water, fully clothed, the second problem revealed itself: just how do you hold up a great sodden, struggling giant of a dog in freezing fast-flowing water? The third part of the rescue was even more difficult: how do you lift a massively heavy 'bear' out of the water on to a river bank which is two or three feet higher than arm's reach?

I think Prince must have read and believed he fitted the Newfoundland breed description, especially the part that said 'excellent swimmer', but he never came to realise that he could not swim at all.

Good Intentions Are Never Enough

Prince never managed to settle down with us. If a window was open he would make his escape through it and then would vanish off the face of the earth for at least half a day: in farming country a big powerful and unpredictable dog on the loose is not a good idea. When he returned he was usually covered in the most foul substances, and of course there was always the worry that we had no idea where he had been.

He got on well with our Labrador, Sugar Ray, and even

better with Tessa the donkey, but he did not seem to be over keen on me. If he thought he was about to be chastised he would back himself into a corner and show the most enormous teeth. It was not just show either – any movement from me would bring about a kind of castanet-clicking as he tried to bite me wherever he could. I tried everything to persuade him that we, as a family, were quite nice and that this was not a bad place to live but my advances fell on unresponsive ears. Fear overcame any chance of trust.

Whatever had happened to him in his previous home or homes had left him beyond rescue. I could manage it now because I have the knowledge gained through a lot of experience but in those days my mind did not travel anywhere near where his problems were. I did not manage to put myself in his place nor did I fully understand his fears.

He was to all intents and purposes a big, tough dog and lots of healthy exercise and affection could not fail to satisfy him. What I did not see was that his fears had to be overcome first.

Nerves have nothing to do with size. I have an enormous Border collie called Barney who reminds me in many ways of Prince: both larger than is normal and both with much more of a nervous disposition than would be expected.

It was much easier to teach Tessa than it ever was to teach Prince. I should have taken my clues from her. She was strong enough to resist any physical attempt to move her in a direction that she did not want to travel but charm and gentle persuasion could move her so easily.

As we had four young children and could not rely on Prince to be gentle and well behaved it became obvious that something other than trying to resettle him had to be done.

I fought off any acceptance of that unpalatable fact for a very long time. I looked to see if I could find a couple without children that could give him a good home but found none.

I hesitated and vacillated about including the story of Prince in this book because it is an account of absolute failure on my part and telling this story that I have kept hidden for so long is painful. Failure is not something to expect in a book about dog training by someone considered to be an expert.

I failed by picking the wrong sort of dog and I failed to offer any kind of suitable remedial training. At the time I probably did not give the problem the sort of thought that I would certainly give it now. I was over-optimistic and irresponsible.

Prince paid the price of my ignorance. He was put to sleep. I was there with him. It hurts to this very day and will continue to be painful. I have never ceased to feel guilty and writing this stirs all of those uncomfortable feelings up again. If I had known then what I know now I could have put it right. This must be the whole world's cry.

I include this story to show that good intentions alone are insufficient tools for the job and that taking time to learn is the least you owe your dog. I include it because I want to try and show the end result of pity and optimism without serious thought about what was really needed.

This is the only failure I have had in a lifetime of training dogs. It would be of some consolation if I could point at some advantages that came out of the situation but I can't, except that I am now much more thoughtful about every aspect of how to get through to a nervous dog. With Prince I got it wrong and an innocent dog paid the price of my incompetence.

If you are planning on resettling a rescue dog look carefully at the implications. You will have to travel with just hope at times but at the start, before love fuzzes up your judgement, ask yourself the type of hard questions that I pointed up earlier: what the breed is suited for, whether it will suit you and your family and your lifestyle, how much time and effort you have to spend on training and exercise, and so on.

It is better to travel with a map than it is without one, even if the only thing it tells you is where the journey should end.

I have probably let more than a few people down in my lifetime but that does not hurt anywhere near as much as my failure to rescue Prince.

Chapter Twenty-seven

For Queen and Country

In the late fifties when I had black hair and looked less like Father Christmas, I spent three years as a guest of Her Majesty's Forces at Aqaba. The British army occupied the slopes of a nine-mile wide *wadi* (valley) that led into deep, inhospitable desert at its northerly end and the palm-fringed beaches of the Gulf of Aqaba, an arm of the Red Sea, at the other. In ancient times this was a caravan resting place, at that time it was a buffer between Jordan and Israel.

We lived in tents, side-flaps wide open during the hot summer months, flaps rolled down against the cold of winter and yes, the desert can be cold. But in summer it was so hot that if you tried to cross a patch of sand in bare feet it would burn so that hopping was the only way. From my tent I could see mountains, sea and the stony, sandy desert.

Beyond the tents, the only more permanent structures were the regimental offices, the cookhouse and the thunder boxes. Some wit, probably a long time ago, described the primitive toilets the army constructed in rough and remote country as thunder boxes. Let me tell you how ours was made and then you can decide if the humorist's choice of name was apt.

First, on the edge of the regiment's compound against the lower slopes of the mountains that protected the camp's rear boundary, an enormous hole had been dug in the desert sand and rock. It was so big that explosives must have played a part in its making. As is the case with an iceberg's mass under water, there will be more happening below than above ground so the word 'enormous' is an understatement of some note. Next, over the top of the pit a wood and corrugated iron hut had been built, inside which was a long box with toilet-seat-sized holes cut in it. Ours had six holes which was not too generous when I remember how many people had to share them. Finally, the holes were capped with hinged flaps.

Once built the life of the thunder box truly begins. There obviously is much organic activity and unwanted vagrants such as flies choose this place as their ideal environment. I hope that I have managed to describe the scene with a degree of refinement.

Visiting the place, though necessary, was not looked on as a pleasant experience though, once there, long conversations were not unusual. The seasoned soldier would enter and open and slam the flaps on all the toilet compartments he did not intend to use in a futile attempt to fool the host of flies that lived in the near darkness of this hellish, oven-hot, underworld. Hell hath no fury like a thunder box. Needless to say, we all became very familiar with the place.

Search and Rescue

One day, when several of us were sitting there putting the world to rights we heard a noise quite foreign in a dreadful place like this. It sounded for all the world like the crying of a baby (or babies) and it went on long enough for us to be sure that something (or some things) were down below. We lifted the lids to see but it was too dark. Torches were found and shone down into the pit and after much sweeping of the area with the beams the light picked up the reflected glow of, we were pretty sure, three pairs of eyes.

Even a mountaineer – wearing an oxygen mask to keep out the stench – would not be able to scale the walls unaided. We went to look for a rope and after a time returned with one that had seen better days but looked up to the job, just.

The next difficulty was that none of us was slim enough to climb through the holes. We went on our third search, this time with a special brief to find a thin and willing soldier: I could ponder for some time on whether thin was more important than willing. Eventually we found a very thin and passionately willing volunteer. The rope was fastened around his waist, then he wriggled and squeezed through the opening directly above the eyes we had seen and we began lowering him. We shone our torches through adjacent openings so that we might see if he was going in the right direction.

Then calamity! The rope went slack and there was a noise best not described. Then, a long silence. We called out to him but no answer came. I remember the alarm I felt and the looks on the other soldier's faces – the feeling of helplessness. Had we put an end to someone's life in an absolutely awful way?

After an age, from the black hole a muffled call came which included the words 'help', 'rope' and several unprintable words best left whence they were delivered.

Luckily, one of our team had shown some foresight and, meantime, had brought back a brand-new rope from the quartermaster's store. After what seemed like an age but was probably only minutes the new rope had been lowered and the victim (or should I say hero) had secured it around his waist.

As you can imagine, hauling him up was both heavy and disgusting. The torch beam picked him up but he was not recognisable. His arms were raised above his head and when he came into clearer view we could see why. On top of his head he held three puppies. He had put them there to make them safe and kept his hands above his head to keep them there. They had scrabbled and scratched his face into furrows from brow to chin.

We set about the long, long process of washing both man and puppies, and of course the rope which had to be returned to the stores. And then we washed ourselves. Not much dinner was eaten that evening.

With time to think we all fully appreciated what our comrade had done and how brave and caring he had been.

He never went short of friends after his loving, compassionate and totally unselfish achievement; in fact, he became a most popular soldier.

Even though it was against all army rules we kept the puppies and looked after them until they were big enough to look after themselves. The puppies were 'primitive' which in this use means virtually unchanged since the origin of their kind, they were feral – wild dogs. As we were just nine miles from the Israeli border they could have been Canaan dogs.

When they grew up they were medium size, creamy coloured and ideally suited in a camouflage sense for life in a sandy desert. Sometimes these dogs are called pi- or pye-dogs, piad or pariah dogs. Pariah is the Tamil word for the untouchable caste and in English means outcast.

The Great Escape

Three of our company each took a puppy and mine grew rapidly, fuelled by all sorts of good, plain, food from the cookhouse. She allowed me to make a fuss of her in a very limited way and would sit within the confines of the concrete base that formed the edges of our tent home but was slightly remote and would not sit very close to me. Preferring to sit and gaze into the distance, she appeared to have her mind on desert while her body (for the time being) chose the safety of the tent. I think, with me, she was simply biding her time. With little imagination I named her Pi and we lived together for four months or so before it became obvious that she would really like to be somewhere else.

When I think back I remember that Pi did not bark or

make many other noises; in fact a wagging tail was a rarity. She did come in response to me squatting and holding my arms out and she did follow me if I was travelling toward the open desert but Pi would not come with me if I was heading for any sort of centre of human business.

She followed me as a puppy would have followed a parent rather than the frisky, gambolling way a puppy follows a human. She was matter-of-fact and there was no room for anything except the serious business of practising for survival.

The army, in general, had started to clamp down on the keeping of these wild dogs and when we heard that they were shooting them in other camps my fellow soldiers and I decided to try and resettle our dogs as quickly as we could.

The only official way out of the camp was through the main gate past the guard room and three soldiers with dogs would not have got far. I can't for one moment imagine that the regiment did not know that there were wild dogs being kept at the camp but parading them openly would have been begging trouble.

At the crack of dawn we wriggled under the coils of barbed wire (as the army had taught us) and softly called the dogs to follow, then made our way along the scree slopes of the mountains. We walked for some time to put distance between the army camp and the dogs until we came to a sand and scrub valley that looked ideally suitable for them.

It was strange because the dogs watched us go but made no attempt to follow. I think they knew that this was where they were meant to be. Even when we were out of sight of where we had left them, we kept looking back expecting to see heads looking over slopes toward us.

We had left as much water and food as we could carry but it would not have lasted for very long and we obviously worried about them. I went back several times in the weeks that followed taking both food and water and saw them, still together, and looking quite content.

It took a long time before I actually thought about how they had ended up in the thunder box. I can only imagine that the reason I was slow to catch on was because I did not want to face up to what had probably happened.

At first I thought that perhaps their mother had dug her nest on the edge of the pit and that, somehow, the puppies had fallen in but then I realised that far more likely someone had thrown them in to get rid of them. For anyone who loves dogs or has any feeling whatsoever for other forms of life this kind of cruelty is unimaginable.

As we go through life we realise that there are some pretty heartless monsters out there. Thank goodness there are others who will go to almost any lengths to save rather than destroy. Even being prepared to be lowered into a pit so foul as to be compared to hell itself to rescue three puppies. If you, 'hero' are still out there and have a dog or dogs of your own, as I am absolutely sure you will, I salute you!

And yes, I do remember your name but that is between you and me and, of course, our maker.

Chapter Twenty-eight

The Guide Man

An old man sits at the breakfast table with his grand-children. He is telling them a story from memory. His breakfast was eaten with gusto and very much enjoyed. Every single mouthful of egg, bacon, mushroom and brown toast with butter was savoured and now the jokes and funny stories flow, much to the enjoyment of the children who laugh until they cry.

The old man is at the centre not only of his world but also at the hub of the others who sit lovingly close to him. It is a perfect tableaux except the old man cannot see it or his fellow players because he is blind.

He remembers what a smile looks like and how good it

feels, and he can sense the good feelings in the room and understands, appreciates and loves all that is going on for this is his family. Those that can see are blind to his blindness. Their feelings toward him are as they have always been.

He misses his sight beyond imagining. He still stands at the bedroom window as he has always done to 'see' the view but, of course, he cannot see it. He must ask others to read the newspaper to him and there are many other deep frustrations in his life. He looks in the mirror, still, but there is no one and nothing there, yet he knows that all is as it should be.

What he can do is play the scene back from a memory crammed with pictures. He can smell the mown grass and the May blossom and he knows pretty well how it looks. He cannot see the love that is sent his way but he can surely feel it and it warms him. The world, though frustrating, is still full of treasures.

If someone suggested putting him down what would your reaction be? Should the ethics vary between human and dog?

My dear little Fadey has, as you know, lost her sight. It happened quickly. Suddenly she started to walk into things. Before any sign of failing sight was apparent she was ill and did not have the strength to even lift her head. She would lie still all day, even when water and food was taken to her. Each day I expected the very worst but she struggled on. I could see that she was not in pain but just seemed exhausted. She did eat every day and at least her appetite remained keen.

As she lay on her cushion I looked at her for some small sign that she knew I was there. I lifted her front paw off the ground, trying to gauge her strength; it was floppy, all vibrancy gone. I even tested the other dogs' paws when they were sleeping to see if they felt so devoid of any sign of energy.

I sat in her kennel at night and prayed for her over and over again. I looked at myself and wondered how I could be like this: I was acting like a child; during my training for the priesthood I had studied theology and philosophy and understood both. Of course, I realised that this was one unavoidable ingredient in the loving relationship between human and dog: there is life and there is death. What appeared to be happening now was natural, in the way of things, to be expected. Logic and reason told me all of this but the information was worthless. My head knew but my heart was not ready to accept any of it. The old man was a little boy again hoping, wishing, and praying for just one more chance.

She did not move much at the beginning but I could see that she could smell, hear and sense what was going on around her. The other dogs were more sensitive toward her than I would have expected and moved carefully when close by. A couple of weeks went by and, very gradually, Fadey started to get a little stronger but the improvement was so slight and so gradual as to be almost imperceptible. The first sign was when I noticed that she knew that I was there and obviously valued and took great comfort from my close, reassuring presence.

At exercise time I carried her out across the fields, stumbling as the other dogs danced inconsiderately around my feet, and we kept to the same routines we have always had hoping that something remembered and meaningful would reactivate her determination to live. When I could carry her no further I would gently set her down in the shade under an apple tree on a blanket of long, cool grass. I still had to carry her down the corridor to her bed – and guess I always will.

Now, she lifts her head when she hears my voice and shows signs with little touches of her nose on my hand that eloquently tell me how very special our relationship is. At bed-time I sit down on her duvet, as close as I can comfortably get, and gently stroke her and talk. I start by saying, 'I remember you when you were a little puppy—' and then speak about all of the events in her life: when she was a mum and had a litter of playing puppies that looked just like her. I tell her what a lovely mother she was and reflect on moments of our lives together and, almost hoping, that maybe God can hear our conversation and that he will help us and make a miracle.

I remember little, unimportant things like her chasing the bristles of the broom we used to sweep out the kennels at the theme park in Devon. And I remember my throw-away line that always amused the audiences at our demonstrations: after giving each dog a wonderful build up and telling about all the clever things it could do and what language it worked in, I would come to Fadey's introduction, 'And now, Fadey, who never takes any notice of any language known to man or beast.'

Of course it was totally untrue – well, not the whole truth, and now I feel guilty for using it. Fadey did not respond to spoken or whistle commands but was always first in the right place at the right time. I used to think that her intuition was so good that, somehow, she could copy the actions of the other dogs almost before they had actually moved.

Then we had a video made so that the skill of my dogs

could still be appreciated long after we had gone and when I watched the completed version for the first time I realised, to my huge surprise, that Fadey shaped the whole demonstration. She set the distance between me and the dogs and varied it according to the size of the arena. She read my body language at the same time as reading the slightest movement from any one of the other eight dogs that were working with her. So, contrary to my cheap, point-scoring, introductory joke, she understood every single word – whatever language it was spoken in – but chose to act on it in her own fashion.

Do you remember, I said earlier, that I once did a show without her and watched the demonstration fall to pieces – it had no form, no shape, no discipline. Even then I did not fully realise why and put it down to an off day for me, or the dogs, or both. Wrong! Wrong! Wrong!

In my mind I draw parallels between various misunderstandings of intelligence made by my father about me and by me about other people. It is a failure of understanding by the one who judges. It is as if virtue is in reaching a decision even though the conclusion is totally inaccurate. I wish they had not happened, but they did.

Routine, Anticipation and Love

The reasons I have included this story are many. Elsewhere I stress the importance of having a routine and sticking faithfully to it.

Fadey's predicament reinforces the importance of routine because when she was fit and well it allowed her, and all of my other dogs, to know what was coming next. The dogs live in a framework that they can safely rely upon and which never leaves them wondering. Dinner comes at this time, walks always at the same time, grooming, bed and all other things to a schedule that is easily understood. Now that Fadey is disadvantaged I can see that the routine still helps and reassures her. It gives her a structure for each day that must be more comfortable to live within.

Another reason this story is included is because it further validates and adds another dimension to my method of training in *layers*. Because I use body language, the spoken word and whistle I have a range of signals to draw on that can still be understood by the disadvantaged dog – be that physically or mentally. In Fadey's case, for example, a whistle is used so that she can locate where I am and walk toward the sound. The body language is used with the dogs that can see and are in danger of running into her and, because such signals are silent, there is no risk of disturbing or alarming Fadey.

When I started training, I realised that dogs can go deaf or blind in old age and that commands or instructions can be used to guide and reassure as well as serving the main purpose which is to instruct.

My training method is based on my anticipation of what might happen and I try to prepare for every contingency my imagination is capable of.

If, for example, you recognise the fact that your dog *might* run away, you can build in training that minimises that possibility. If you take into account all of the things that *could* happen and put training in place before they do, then you will have taken the wise course. Thinking about what to do after the event is too late, prevention is the key.

If your dog goes deaf and all you have are sound signals then you will not be able to communicate. Should its sight fail then body signals will be to no avail.

There are two more reasons for telling you Fadey's story. The first is the most important of them all and that is to emphasise that the best fuel to run a dog on is love.

> *There is no dog that is so troubled*
> *that love cannot cure it.*

The very last reason – because your dog will grow old – is that you should be loving to your dog today.

A teacher of religion said, 'Repent a day before your death.'

His students asked, 'But how do we know when the day of our death will come?'

The teacher replied, 'You will not know, so you had better start today!'

My view of dogs differs from most other people's. They are not just pets nor are they slaves to my will. And they are not just friends but best friends.

We humans are made from the same timeless matter that constitutes the whole universe, for the blink of an eye it resides in our shape and then it is gone to reside somewhere else. Dogs are the same but matter formed in a different shape for a different purpose. Good fortune, luck, chance or intention has enabled us to live with them for a short time: we can do it well or we can do it badly. I also believe that imagination, love, kindness and all of the noble attributes we are capable of will last forever and will come together again somehow and somewhere. My great hope is that this coming together will be whole and complete.

We all have dreams, some of them recur. Mine is a visual one with no words. I see a field, the biggest field there has ever been; it goes on forever, has no end. It could not be crossed, however many lifetimes were used in trying. It is green with cool, thick grass and shady places. Figures move across this sylvan landscape. Some have four legs and some have two. I recognise them. There are no demands, no duties, no destination and no time. Each moment contains the joy and the freshness of the first moment.

Would I swap what we have now for this? No, not yet. Nor do I want Fadey to step over into this other place and have to wait for me and for the others. Selfishly, I want her with me.

Over the course of another three weeks she regained a little more of her strength. Now she can walk all the way to and, with a sit down, back from the training field. I keep her on a lead until we are out in the middle where there are no trees that she might bump into then I release her. I see the recognition of freedom on her face and note that she heard the click of the lead's clip. She even runs, in a fashion, and I try to guess which direction she might go so that I can arrive there first.

I still have her – perhaps for a little, perhaps for a lot more time.

When I sit on the grass and watch her putting her head

up and sniffing the air, sensing where the other dogs are, I realise that our prayers always seem to include the word please but seldom thank you. Which could mean that we only truly believe when we are desperate and want something and, perhaps, can find nowhere else to turn. Some people, when whatever it was works out well, then put the credit for the gift somewhere else. What strange creatures we are.

There are people who pray for some outcome or another, and receive it, and then have little faith about where the answer came from. I *know* where it came from and I thank you even though I know my next prayer will, as always, start with please . . .

Chapter Twenty-nine

Billy and Millie

I shall have to tiptoe delicately through this story because new owners still have contact with old ones and I would like to save both embarrassment and aggravation. No names, no pack drill!

If I had not found a Border collie lying in the road twenty-two years ago, I would have chosen a West Highland white terrier, better known as a Westie. Maureen and I had planned to go and see one the day after we found Annie. I have always liked these independent little characters. It was not to be, and though I do not regret for one moment the fact that a Border collie got to us first I have not ceased to admire these handsome little dogs.

This is the story of Billy, a Westie who started life in a very grand way. A family, originally from the Middle East and by then living in one of the choicest areas of England's capital city, wanted a dog – or to be more accurate, the family's little boy wanted one.

Nothing unusual about that except that the family were Muslims and the dog does not rate highly on their scale of desirables. The Prophet Muhammad, according to the Sunni tradition, did not like dogs. It is said that angels will not enter a house that contains a dog and dogs are not allowed to be kept as pets unless their function is to guard, herd or work, or to guide a blind person but, even then, close contact is frowned upon. Dogs are considered to be 'ritually unclean'. Equally, though, Islamic law sets out a clear ban on unkind treatment to animals.

The little boy lived in an environment where the rules about dogs would most likely have prevented him from understanding the nature of the creature so the relationship was, at best, distant and totally lacking in understanding. Billy, of course, was not aware of the thinking that shaped his life and nor probably at the beginning of the relationship was the little boy who owned him.

It is safe to say that Billy's life was not a happy one. The family that owned him were only in this country for three months of every year so for the other nine months Billy's life was 'maintained' by an ever-changing group of people allowing little chance of any permanent and loving relationships.

A poor little rich dog. Poverty in the midst of great wealth!

The house in London was patrolled by security guards, some European and some Middle Eastern. Among them there might have been a dog lover or two and they would have taken Billy for walks but he would have come home to a gloomy room in the basement away from the family. On one occasion he was shut in a garage and left there for two weeks by a guard that obviously had no time for dogs. Obviously water and food were supplied but not human company.

Finally, this sad story takes a better turn. A lady who worked as an administrator for the family decided to take early retirement and move to the country and, to cut a long story short, she took Billy with her.

'The boss man said I could take Billy as I obviously loved him and the boss woman was glad to see him go as she was tired of hearing him bark and generally having him around,' the new owner told me.

Together they moved to a little country house and suddenly Billy had the attention he deserved. There was just one voice to listen to – and this one actually talked to him – and just one person's routine to get used to. There were walks in the countryside and a loving life to enjoy.

Even with this huge improvement in his life Billy took three years to cheer up and become the real country dog he is today. Now, says his new owner, 'He chases squirrels and swims in every bit of water he can find, and has a black Labrador as his best friend.' She says Billy has become a confident little chap who is very loyal and loves all children, quite the opposite of the way he'd been in London.

Two Types of Neglect

I met Billy for the first time at a photo shoot in a village near where he and his new owner live. In all, there were five dogs ready to pose for the pictures we were going to take. As I watched the dogs joining in the excitement I noticed two that were not as unreservedly at ease with the busy goings-on. One was Billy and the other was a black Labrador called Millie.

At this point I knew nothing of their previous lives but I could discern the scars that had been indelibly inflicted on both dogs and it is only because I asked their owners to tell me all about them that I am able to retell their stories here.

Both dogs came up to me with tails wagging (just) but both were slightly suspicious, both holding back as though they wanted to take a really good and thorough look at this strange man before making any kind of judgement. There was a definite reticence and temporary suspension of the usual behaviour I'd expect from a confident, happy dog.

Billy became remote and almost invisible, as though he was reasoning that if he couldn't be seen then he couldn't get into any kind of trouble. He mentally absented himself from any social interaction and made a very good job of it, which, considering the enormous amount of practice he had been forced to have, was not really surprising.

Millie had the saddest eyes I have ever seen and she used them to implore me to be gentle with her. It was if we were able to speak with each other and that our conversation was fully understood by both of us. I have never seen such a vulnerable look in a dog's eyes before, or been so instantly attracted.

So, from the little white dog that for most of its life had been largely ignored and made invisible came an attempt to achieve even more invisibility: this had become his defence mechanism and was how he coped at times of stress. And from the Labrador that had been very roughly treated came a plea for gentleness, even though this had not worked with her previous owners. Here, then, are two forms of neglect – one might almost say opposing in nature – both caused by humans who had no understanding.

The one ingredient that is ever present with people who treat their dogs badly is an overdeveloped blindness toward the needs of the dog they live with.

Billy lived in a vacuum, a desert, a sterile, cold place where love was completely absent. Millie had had too much attention and most of it had been completely the wrong kind.

Deaf, Dumb and Blind to the Problem

Let me tell you about Millie: she lived with a family that thought she was some kind of moving toy. They would probably be shocked if they knew that I was being so critical of them because they would not see what I am saying. The parents must have been a little like the three monkeys, you know the ones: one covers its eyes, another its ears and the other its mouth.

They saw their children jumping all over Millie and riding her like a donkey, but they covered their eyes. They must have heard Millie yelp when more than once the door was carelessly slammed on her tail, but they covered their ears. They obviously covered their mouths, too, because their children did not learn how to be kind to their dog – no one insisted that they should be.

Millie now lives with a couple who understand how to treat dogs properly and she has improved but the uncertainty with which she greets each new experience is understandably still there.

When we lived in Devon my wife took on a consultancy job to raise money for a private school. One part of her job was to encourage parents to come to an open day so that they could see for themselves where much-needed improvements could be made. Maureen rang the mother of a pupil to invite her only to be told that she was too busy and coming to the open day would interfere with her plans adding, 'that is why we sent him in the first place'.

There is an ancient religion in what used to be called Persia called Zoroastrianism which still has a following. In essence, Zoroastrians believe that there is a force for good and another for evil and that both struggle for the possession of our souls. This has always appealed to me greatly because it so accurately reflects what I see in the world. I would add the thought that there is usually a good person, unknowingly, waiting to correct the damage caused by a bad one.

If you already have, or are about to get, a rescue dog it is worth remembering that the dog you take might well have suffered similar things to both Billy and Millie but that you probably will not know about them. The people who threw out such dogs would not think them important enough to have a story, let alone bother to tell it.

One meaning of myopic is showing a lack of foresight or long-term planning; blind can mean being unable or unwilling to see; blindfolded means to be wearing a blindfold – a piece of cloth tied over the eyes to prevent the wearer from seeing. All of these words come close to what I am trying to say, but not quite close enough. I shall invent one of my own: blindmindfold. Though clumsy, it will do nicely. It means an insensitive brain prevents the eyes from seeing.

The key to resettling any dog is the ability to see. I said right at the start of this book, and since, how important it is to see life from the dog's point of view. Looking carefully at your dog is vital because what you observe will inform the methods you use to train and resettle your dog.

Each of the new owners of Billy and Millie have achieved much through love, consideration and reassuring routines but, and most of all, because they took a lot of time to look, to empathise and to understand.

Chapter Thirty

Dogs Like Happy Endings

A year on, and it is the sort of March that comes in like a lamb rather than a lion. I can feel the coming spring either because my nose tells me it is on its way or by some other sense that our prehistoric ancestors took for granted and that we do not even know we own. Thank goodness that the veneer called civilisation is not too thick and that out in the fresh air the animal in us can still read the signs. Spring is on its way, something almost tangible – though I cannot describe it – tells me so.

I am sitting in my study, in front of a computer, writing, and planning more words than actions for this day. I'm in the middle of my own little world when a voice breaks in:

'Someone to see you,' Maureen calls from the kitchen.

'Who is it?' I ask, hoping that whoever it is their communication will be short and sweet so that I can get back to my work.

'It's Lindsay. He wants to know if you'd like to go and help move some ewes and lambs.'

Mention ewes, lambs and move in one sentence and my mind becomes enthusiastically active, the next word in that chain of thought is dog. Now you are talking!

The muddy quad bike was originally red and, once upon a time, had chrome bump bars. Now it wears nature's camouflage and could be completely invisible to the human eye if it were parked in the middle of a spring field. Lindsay is nearly as muddy as his quad and Floss his sheepdog is more so. Both of them are as skinny as pipe cleaners, constantly on the go – the sheep farmer and his dog must burn off a lot of fat. They are a kind of statement about a way of life that, apart from the quad, has not changed that much in a hundred years

'Who are you going to bring?' Lindsay asks. 'Misty?'

I think about it. I know why he is suggesting Misty; she is slow and steady and not likely to threaten the tiny lambs. I produce a gesture halfway between a nod of agreement and 'I'm not so sure—' the intention being to confuse. I say nothing more. I plump for Ceri – knowing I was always going to – but, somehow, still surprised at my bravery, or foolhardiness, in making *this* particular choice. After all, Misty is the experienced dog.

In Devon they would say, 'Yom bravey.' At first, when I received such a compliment I felt flattered; not a bad thing to be brave. But later, much later, I realised that what had made me puff my chest out with pride was actually a frank comment about the stupidity of foolhardiness. Taking Ceri was very close to both stupid and foolhardy, but hunches often fly to great heights in the gap between folly and inspiration.

Ceri has never seen a lamb close up, or far away for that matter, or experienced the fierce love a ewe has for its infant that makes it attack the dog to keep it away from that tender creature. The nearest to frontline action that Ceri has come is staring, mesmerised, at our rams behind the safety of a sturdy sheep fence during feeding time and being hypnotised by our ducks.

I know that what I am about to do will either prove me right – and show me as I'd like to be seen, the wise old shepherd – or make me look like an inexperienced amateur. I have an instinct that feels very much like certainty that this will provide the 'magic button', the great step forward I have been looking for in Ceri's journey toward graduation as a sheepdog. Deep down, in a strange sort of way, I trust him. He is not the mad dog he used to be – I have seen evidence.

'See you down there,' Lindsay shouts, revving off down our drive, the knobbly tread on his fat tyres throwing small lumps of mud and grass into the air. When he has turned the corner and gone completely, I set off to pick up Ceri from his kennel.

It is hard to separate him from the other dogs who are all keen to come and do their stuff. Susie looks at me in disgust as though I have made a really bad choice. Her expression suggests absolute contempt for the silly shepherd choosing an out-and-out novice. She thinks that I ought to have taken her – and by the look on some of the dogs' faces they, also, are absolutely sure that it ought to have been them. I am sure Susie is muttering something rude about my lack of judgement.

Ceri's Big Day

I pat the front seat of my Jeep just once and Ceri is there in a flash. I think he has a clue about the sort of thing we are about to do. He knows for certain that it looks exciting.

We drive about a mile along a winding country lane between farms before we hit the rough farm track where the shock absorbers start absorbing significant shocks and I shift into four-wheel drive. We bump and sway across the fields, ever deeper into the valley, throwing spectacular curtains of muddy water into the air until we see Lindsay sitting on his quad bike. He sits as though on a trusty steed rather than a machine – all he needs to complete the picture is a Stetson and a fringed, buckskin jacket.

We leave our vehicles and take our dogs across the muddy fields on foot, me with the surprisingly professional Ceri and Lindsay with his youngest dog, Ben.

Lindsay tells me what he plans to do, waving his arms to show where he wants his sheep moved to; these ones from here to there, the sheep on the hill to the valley. A good shepherd can be recognised not by skills alone but by the clarity of his intentions. Nothing is more frustrating than someone who is woolly about what has to be done and the order it should be done in. 'Woolly' is what sheep are.

Lindsay and I can read each other and, as they flank in

opposite directions to encircle the flock, I notice that the dogs can, too.

'Who did you bring?' Lindsay asks – farmers always ask *who*, not *which* dog. In fact, even fox and badger are prefaced with 'Mr' in Devon, and similarly in Wales. He is looking down at master Ceri but doesn't recognise him: to everyone but their owner, all sheepdogs tend to look alike.

'Ceri,' I say, trying just by tone of voice and the throwaway nature of the delivery to suggest that this is no big deal. If I forget the 'master' then maybe it will not attract as much concern. I could swear a small frown momentarily passed across Lindsay's face, like a fast-moving cloud.

Ceri Rounds 'em Up

In the first field are fifty or so ewes with strong lambs born two-to-three weeks earlier. I make hissing noises to Ceri and he moves, very slowly, toward the little group of mums and babies on the brow of the hill. His body is hunched low to the ground in that classic pose that shouts 'good sheepdog', and always fills me with satisfaction and great joy. This pose is proof positive that Ceri knows what his long line of ancestors did – a folk, or rather dog, memory.

For the first ten minutes that we work he is not quite sure what he's meant to be doing but, nevertheless, gives a very good impersonation of a dog that does. But once the first bunch of sheep is gathered and we start to slowly drive them toward their destination his confidence and awareness grow in leaps and bounds.

I notice that he is gentle and kind, and very steady.

Sometimes, when the tiny lambs are confused by the mêlée they will dash up to the dog as though it was their mother. When they run to Ceri he keeps his mouth firmly shut, teeth hidden, and gently but firmly ushers them back to their mother's side. His kindness comes as a revelation to me. I had not imagined him to own such a great share of this quality.

In the next field there are lambs so small and unsteady on their legs that we have to move them very slowly. They are just days old, and the dried string of umbilical cord still hangs stiffly from their navels.

Ceri performs each task like a master and responds instantly to my calls.

He is more intelligent and much more suited to his task than I had realised.

Even my hand signals indicating him to flank to the left or the right are immediately and sensitively acted on – or was he taking the decision before I even realised there was one to be made? He even manages to hold a little group of sheep in a hollow to give us time to see which lamb belongs to which ewe; he is gently nudging lambs back to their mothers. Ewes and lambs must be driven carefully in order to keep the right babies with the right mums: it is testing for both shepherd and dog. When we miss two or three sheep hidden in a fold of the land, Ceri goes back to find them and the glimpse of black and white informs me of his position and reassures me that he is doing his job gently and properly.

After a couple of hours we have finished moving the

various groups from one field to another and all the sheep are now on better grass. Back on his quad, Lindsay sits and reviews what we have done. He is proud of his young dog – Ben has made great progress he tells me.

Then he asks about Ceri, remarking that the dog has obviously done this before. When I tell him that this was his very first time he raises his eyebrows in surprise and utters a one-word appraisal: 'Impressive.'

The Shepherd and His Dog: Satisfaction Guaranteed

As we walk back to the Jeep Ceri is looking at me in a different way: he is confident, he has suddenly grown up. If a dog can be proud then that is what he is. I pat his head and tell him how good he was.

We get into the Jeep but, this time, I put Ceri in the back – he is very, very muddy. I take a last look at the landscape. The sky is duck-egg blue with smudges of cloud that look as though half-an-hour in the washing machine would benefit them. The land falls in a series of rounded hills toward ground by the river, the 'bottoms'. The tide is in and the high, wide River Usk sparkles as small star shapes of light shimmer on the tops of the muddy-brown waves. On the far bank the land rises steeply in wooded slopes which seem to reach the very sky.

Meanwhile, from the mouth of the valley a heavy, wet, slate-grey cloud with touches of purple rolls ever closer like a wide, solid curtain: it is going to rain.

Ceri and I drive up the steep hill on the unmade track

splashing, happily, through small muddy pools, both of us well and truly content with a job well done.

I can see his face in the driver's mirror –
his pink tongue is out and he is smiling;
he looks like a different dog.

I don't need any special body-language skills to see that he is fulfilled and content with the task he has accomplished.

The relationship that a shepherd shares with his dog is a special one. There is of course the delight you feel when your dog delivers in the field the promise it has shown in training but the very best part is knowing how well the partnership worked. There is an eloquent silence at such moments that needs no interpretation, we are at one, the thoughts of dog and man are known to each other and the moment is magical.

Bury me with my shepherd's crook and a whistle around my neck. And make sure that my clothes are not my best and have mud on them so that when I get to where I am going they will know where my place is.

The windscreen wipers beat like a metronome and work hard to clear the muddy water from the screen. I reflect on the fact that my days of swiftly striding up steep hills are probably numbered and the realisation makes the recollection of all those times that I've been able to do it more treasured.

A very pleased Ceri is put back in his run, his companions sniff his black, muddy legs with huge interest as if to say, 'You lucky thing, we know where you have been.' In my wildest fancy I like to imagine that dogs speak to each other with the accents of their birthplace. All of mine are Devon dogs. Today, for certain, it would be an interesting conversation.

I put a huge armful of the most fragrant hay into Ceri's bed and thank him quietly lest the others should hear and be envious. He drinks deeply from the bucket of cool well water in his yard and then stretches out, full-length, on his bed of hay and within seconds he is sound asleep. He will surely have the most pleasant dreams.

Maureen is in the kitchen. I leave my disgusting boots in the porch and drop my filthy jeans outside the door.

'How did he do?' she asks. Her expression suggests that she already knows and just needs confirmation.

A Pleasure and a Privilege

I tell my or, rather, our story and she nods repeatedly and enthusiastically throughout, knowing how important the verdict was and no doubt remembering the sad, nervous dog we rescued and brought back home nearly five years before.

I tell her that Ceri is a natural, a canine genius born to the task. And as I speak I know that this afternoon will be always in my mind's eye, in my collection of moving pictures. In my head, I shall play it back a million times and each time it will bring back feelings of pride and warm satisfaction. Ceri will move confidently, purposefully and smoothly through the film in my mind until my dying day. It is my reason for living, a kind of justification.

When God plays the film back He will know what we did, He will hear the music and feel the harmony and maybe, just maybe, He will like this small thing that we have done.

I go and sit on the stone step of our front porch. I look out across the valley and the river to the wooded slopes that form the next mountain. On the mountaintop is a folly built, so I've been told, by a rich man to pray in. He chose a very good spot for his quiet contemplation.

To the right of the step where I sit is a stone statue of a Pharaoh hound that Maureen and I bought in a garden centre. It is almost as big as some of my Border collies. The moment I placed it by the porch it ceased to be just an ornament but became, instead, a focal point that never fails to remind me of the dogs that I have lived with. Even though its eyes are cold, grey stone its gaze suggests that it is patiently waiting for its human to come home, as though they might walk down the path at any moment. It does not matter that it is a Pharaoh hound and not a Border collie, or that it is made of stone, because it symbolises the essence of our friend the dog and of a secure resting place.

I look out over the beautiful valley and fondle the ears of the stone dog and the longer I sit, and the longer I think, the more I remember the dogs that I have loved and lost: Annie, lost then found; dear little Grumble, who died too young to have the chance to shine; Wing, who spent his early years running away and his later years performing like a genius. And Mollie, the mother of my pack, who was so strong-minded that she even tried to shepherd death itself.

I have led a privileged life working with good friends out in God's creation and for all those manifold gifts I say, thank you. Amen

Postscript

The Sermon

In church, children and adults alike would ask me about their pets: Do they just live and then die? Is this the end? I had always replied to questions of this sort by saying that, logically, heaven will be complete rather than lacking in anything as its existence is based on complete love. But I could see by the questioners' faces that this was only ever partly heard.

It is in the nature of people to not hear an answer whereas a story will be listened to. I wanted my message to get through so I wrote it down as a story and delivered it as a sermon which was heard and appreciated.

I retell my sermon here as I believe it will make a fitting end to this book.

The old shepherd leaned on the kitchen windowsill of the old Devon longhouse.

Behind him, in the darkness away from the light of the window, there was an ancient solid-fuel Aga with its upper shelf piled high with underwear, some still worn, drying, and some long forgotten. In the middle of the room stood a plain, pine table big enough to seat a harvesting team of at least eight men. The floor was laid with flagstones and the walls were smooth with generations of white paint. On either side of the Aga old armchairs that should have been retired long ago still offered saggy-seated comfort to a tired shepherd.

Outside, the sky was grey, heavy and louring.

He stood there for a long time, not so much looking at the sky but remembering his life, here, on the farm. He had lived here man and boy and every corner of every field and every barn was holy in his memory.

He remembered when he had asked the love of his life that all-important question and how he had expected the answer to be 'no'. He had waited until they had walked the length of the lane before he had nervously delivered the four most important words in the world. On the way back he had whacked the branches of the horse chestnut trees with a stick and shouted with an exuberant joy at the sky itself, 'She said yes, she said yes.'

They had lived in this farmhouse and raised their children here. They had been lovers and best friends.

Suddenly she had become ill. There was no warning. It just came out of the blue. Then she was gone and he was left to try to live without her.

Friends told him that time would heal his wounds but they were wrong. Sometimes he could smell a hint of her perfume, as though she had just walked by, and he would look up half expecting the impossible. Sometimes, for a moment, out of the corner of his eye he would catch just a glimpse of her pale face and dark, thick hair. He would tell himself that it was all in his imagination while hoping against hope that it could be true.

He went back to the breakfast table to finish his now cold egg and toast. He felt a soft nudge on his knee and put his hand down under the table to stroke the dog's head. She would not have been allowed indoors if his wife was still here but he had been so lonely that he had brought the dog inside to live with him.

He looked down and noticed, as if for the first time, the grey of her muzzle and her gun-metal eyes, now clouded. She looked back at him and saw his age.

'You must be as old as me, my love,' he said. 'What is it now, seven of your years to every one of mine?'

She wagged her tail as if she understood every word.

He could see her in his mind's eye, the young dog running across the green July fields, her coat bluey-black and shining in the sun. He could still hear the whistles as though it was happening now. What a poor substitute memory is for the real thing.

He carried his plate and mug to the stone sink and then turned back toward the door.

'Time to go and see they sheep.'

The old dog and the old man went out through the porch as they had done every day for a lifetime. It was as if they were joined by an invisible string.

They crossed the yard and entered the first field. High in the sky the angels shook their wings and the first flakes fell toward the earth. It was no more than a gentle dusting to start with but as they worked their way up toward the moors it came down in great flakes, like goose feathers.

Now it was hard to see where field and sky met. He could hear Lass wheezing and panting as they climbed higher and he was suddenly tired. He took her by her collar and guided her into the lee of bank and hedge and sat down, pulling the dog between his knees and wrapping his great, rough coat around them both for warmth.

The snow lay like a thick, white blanket over the silent landscape. He was tired of struggling and weary of all things. It was to end, here, as it was written in the book. In his mind, night fell and blackness and total silence came.

This could be the end of my story but it is the beginning. He woke in the shadow of a man holding a crook. How could he wake after he was gone? The man was standing in front of him with his back to the sun. The old man was surprised for no one except him and his dog came up to the high moors.

He asked the man, 'Who are you?'

The stranger answered in a voice the old man thought he knew, and would certainly never forget.

'I am a Shepherd too.'

At the sound of the voice, Lass stirred between his knees as though she was waking from the most wonderful sleep. Her ears pricked and she looked down the field as though she had heard something the old man could not hear.

Then she ran as she used to run, like a poem in full flight, kicking the sparkling snowflakes in the air. Her coat added the blue of the sky to its lustrous, shining black – she was young again.

Lass ran past the man with the crook toward a woman

who was walking toward them. The woman had a pale face framed by the thickest, darkest hair. He knew every, lovely inch of her.

Omega . . . or is it Alpha?

Index

Note: Entries may be assumed to refer to rescue as well as other dogs, and to Border collies unless otherwise indicated.

More Non-fiction from Headline

THE DOG WHISPERER

GRAEME SIMS

'I have never met a dog that could not be trained
once the right approach is found'

Graeme Sims's numerous dogs follow his every
command – because they want to. Their eager obedience
is the result of a bond of understanding that means,
in effect, that the extraordinary Graeme Sims can
'speak dog'. Enormously experienced, his revolutionary
but gentle training techniques will help you:

- communicate properly with your dog
- use different commands
- build trust and cooperation
- overcome problems
- choose a breed that suits your lifestyle

Easy to follow, this enlightening and heart-warming book
will prove invaluable to dog lovers everywhere.

NON-FICTION / PETS 978 0 7553 1700 4

REX HARPER

AN OTTER ON THE AGA

Meet the remarkable Rex Harper, a real-life Dr Doolittle . . .

Since opening his first animal sanctuary in the 1950s, Rex has rescued and rehabilitated more than 50,000 creatures.

In this unforgettable memoir, Rex tells the amazing story of his life with animals. He describes how, against the odds, he and his wife Julie built their unique haven in Cornwall, and how their sanctuary became the county's first official RSPCA animal rescue centre.

You'll meet a menagerie of memorable characters including Odin the Machiavellian raven, and One Eye the seemingly indestructible cat.

An Otter on the Aga is a story that will warm – and occasionally break – the hearts of animal lovers everywhere.

NON-FICTION / MEMOIR 978 0 7553 1628 1

AN EAGLE IN THE AIRING CUPBOARD

As another year begins at his animal sanctuary in the Cornish countryside, life remains as unpredictable as ever for RSPCA warden Rex Harper.

On top of the usual influx of battered dogs, unwanted kittens and oil-soaked birds, Rex has to cope with some unusual visitors, from an amorous duck called Pierre to a troublesome tortoise called Tommy.

Adding to his worries, he faces a potentially catastrophic outbreak of illness amongst the animals, a stressful court action against an abusive dog owner, and a crucial inspection.

Will the sanctuary survive its most testing twelve months yet?

NON-FICTION / MEMOIR 978 0 7553 1803 2

DAVID KENNARD

A SHEPHERD'S WATCH

At Borough Farm, on the spectacularly beautiful North Devon Coast, David Kennard and his dogs are embarking on a new shepherding year.

The twelve months ahead will present David and his sheepdogs Greg, Swift, Gail, Fern and Ernie with a never-ending series of challenges: from spring lambing and summertime shearing to rescuing ewes stranded on the Atlantic cliffs and fending off the ever-present threats nature – and the occasional officious farm inspector – has in store for the 850-strong flock.

Part diary of one man and his remarkable dogs, part Herriot-like homage to the countryside and its characters, *A Shepherd's Watch* is that rare thing: a portrait of life that is at once authentic and evocative, warm and compelling.

NON-FICTION / MEMOIR 978 0 7553 1235 X

THE DOGS OF WINDCUTTER DOWN

'There is no good flock without a good shepherd,
and there is no good shepherd without good dogs'

These age-old words of wisdom have always guided Devon sheep farmer David Kennard. But as he battles to save his farm from exctinction, they resonate more loudly – and unexpectedly – than ever. David knows he will be able to rely, as always, on his faithful sheepdogs. But even he is surprised when the dogs – aided and abetted by eccentric newcomer Jake – prove to be Borough Farm's secret weapon . . .

'Perhaps the most honest and restrained first-hand account of modern farming that I know of . . . This author has the rare ability to adopt an outsider's point of view without being patronising . . . The warm togetherness of the family radiates off the page like heat from an Aga, and the detailed descriptions of his work with the dogs pushes this beyond straightforward memoir'
Richard Benson, author of *The Farm*

NON-FICTION / MEMOIR 978 0 7553 1803 2

Now you can buy any of these other bestselling non-fiction titles from your bookshop or *direct from the publisher.*

FREE P&P AND UK DELIVERY
(Overseas and Ireland £3.50 per book)

The Dog Whisperer *Graeme Sims* £7.99
Graeme Sims's detailed, step-by-step instruction book shows you how to communicate properly with your dog and is a definitive guide to effective dog training for dog-owners and dog-lovers everywhere.

An Otter on the Aga *Rex Harper* £7.99
Rex Harper brings to life the story of the incredible animal sanctuary that he and his family spent over forty years building and introduces us to the colourful cast of characters that have become his family.

The Dogs of Windcutter Down *David Kennard* £7.99
The extraordinary story of David Kennard and his five Devon sheepdogs, and the fight to save Borough Farm from extinction.

The Horses in My Life *Monty Roberts* £8.99
World famous horse-gentler tells the stories of those horses he has loved most and learned most from throughout his career.

My Colourful Life: From Red to Amber *Ginger McCain* £7.99
The remarkable life story of the legendary trainer of Red Rum, three-times winner of the Grand National.

Mince Pie for Starters *John Oaksey* £8.99
One of racing's great characters recalls his life in the sport and provides a definitive account of racing since the war in this brilliantly entertaining memoir.

TO ORDER SIMPLY CALL THIS NUMBER

01235 400 414

or visit our website: www.headline.co.uk

Prices and availability subject to change without notice.